MW00622878

the book
your cat
wishes
you would
read

the book
your cat
wishes
you would
read

LUCY HOILE

S

First published in Great Britain in 2023 by Orion Spring
an imprint of The Orion Publishing Group Ltd
Carmelite House, 50 Victoria Embankment
London EC4Y 0DZ

An Hachette UK Company

1 3 5 7 9 10 8 6 4 2

Copyright © Lucy Hoile 2023

The moral right of Lucy Hoile to be identified as
the author of this work has been asserted in accordance
with the Copyright, Designs and Patents Act of 1988.

All rights reserved. No part of this publication may be
reproduced, stored in a retrieval system, or transmitted
in any form or by any means, electronic, mechanical,
photocopying, recording, or otherwise, without the
prior permission of both the copyright owner and the
above publisher of this book.

A CIP catalogue record for this book is
available from the British Library.

ISBN (Hardback) 978 1 3987 2033 6
ISBN (eBook) 978 1 3987 2034 3
ISBN (Audio) 978 1 3987 2035 0

Typeset by Born Group
Printed in Great Britain by Clays Ltd, Elcograf S.p.A.

MIX
Paper from
responsible sources
FSC® C104740

www.orionbooks.co.uk

To Pepper, Parker and Marnie.

Always remember that kind words can change somebody's world, even if that somebody has four legs and a tail. Love you, love you, love you.

Every effort has been made to ensure that the information in this book is accurate. The information may not be applicable in each individual case so it is advised that professional veterinary advice is obtained for specific health matters. Neither the publisher nor author accepts any legal responsibility for any injury or other damage or loss arising from the use of the information in this book.

Contents

INTRODUCTION

If you're here, I like you already. Anyone looking to better understand their cat is a perfect cat caregiver in my eyes. No one knows your cat better than you do, and this book is a window into your cat's world. It will help you see things you may not have noticed before or perhaps look at things a bit differently. It's a companion to help you strengthen that bond and deepen your understanding of feline behaviour.

Don't you think it's strange cats have a reputation for being aloof, fiercely independent and antisocial? That doesn't fit the cats I share my home with. As I sit at my desk, my two companions are, of course, my little cats, Fig and Sparx, who – after the standard amount of wandering all over the keyboard – have settled beside me, Sparx asleep, Fig quietly purring in anticipation that I might pay him some attention – a look, a small word or a scratch behind the ears. Hardly antisocial.

Tarring all cats with the antisocial brush can cause problems. It leads less experienced cat owners to assume they are low-maintenance pets and can essentially take care of themselves. These myths seem to be held even more strongly by those that have never lived with a cat, leading to frustrating conversations like one friend insisting cats should only drink milk (despite being lactose intolerant), and another insisting cats and dogs can't live happily together – essentially gaining all their knowledge of cat behaviour from an episode of *Tom and Jerry*.

We can all agree that cats are an enigma – they are not the easiest creatures to understand. They are fascinating and mysterious, retaining so much of their wild physiology and behaviour, while seemingly slotting in perfectly to domesticated life. Over eight million households in the UK own at least one cat – that's over a quarter of all UK households – many of which have a cherished relationship with them. So why can't they shake the reputation of being antisocial?

It's because, as a species, cat social behaviour is determined by whether they feel they can trust you. Some live successfully as free-roaming feral cats, having little or no contact with people and are totally self-sufficient. These guys really are antisocial – although some wonderful people can carefully tame an individual in genuine need. Others – such as street cats – have some degree of contact with people. And then there are those that completely rely on us to provide their food and a safe place to live. These home-loving cats are rarely truly antisocial, but some people can cause a friendly cat to take a dislike to them by stroking too heavily or spooking them by moving too quickly. Every cat is different, but we need to accept that pet cats are not totally independent – they rely on us for survival and our role is to understand their specific needs and do what we can to meet them.

This book aims to help you do just that. It is about seeing the world from a cat's point of view. It's about empathy. It's about forming a deep understanding of cats' innate drives and motivations; and learning what your individual cat needs based on their genetics, experiences and current environment. When you know this, you know their struggles, what they want and how this influences their behaviour. This can help you understand your cat's more challenging behaviour, why this behaviour has developed and why it persists. It can also help you identify ways to stop it. You can even prevent problems developing later – and, as with most things, prevention is better than cure.

It is not always easy to give your cat everything they need. Life is often hard and busy, and we may have other pressing commitments. After subjecting Fig and Sparx to three children, two house moves and a puppy, I understand. If you find yourself reading the information throughout this book and realising you have made mistakes or misunderstood your cat's behaviour at times, you are not alone. We've all been there and that does not mean you are bad cat caregiver. Cats are renowned for being elusive, yet they have a reputation of being low maintenance and easy to look after. So even the very best and most dedicated carers can get it wrong sometimes, expecting the experience of understanding and living with a cat to be much more straightforward than it actually is.

Whether you're in search of the solution to a particular problem or just looking to build a deeper understanding of cats, this book is a tool to help you feel more confident in understanding his or her needs (I will refer to both males and females interchangeably throughout), and to bring you closer to the pet you clearly care so much about.

Throughout this book you will learn how this previously solitary, wild predator has integrated itself into our homes and hearts. I will take you through the factors that shape a cat's personality and how this influences their behaviour and your relationship. The third and biggest section of this book will help you to understand what your cat needs from you.

They are not so independent as they appear and big problems can arise both for you and your cat if they need more, or something different, than you are currently giving them. We will explore the special ways in which cats feel and think, and how we can provide them with the perfect home environment, minimise stress and be the person they trust most. You will find the answers to questions such as should you let your cat outside? Why should you neuter/ spay? Can your cat live with other animals and how can you make this work?

Above all, this book is a celebration of how wonderful it is to share your life with the beautiful, yet often misunderstood, companion that is the cat. It will help you build a relationship that is sustainable and works for both of you. I am here to help you on your way to becoming the best caregiver you can be for your unique cat and to give them the life they would want if they could choose for themselves. Let's embark on this journey together, to find out what your cat wishes you knew and how this can change what you can do for your cat.

PART ONE

Understanding Your Cat

1

Domestication

Feline domestication – a series of changes in the social behaviour of cats – has resulted in a mutually beneficial relationship between cats and humans. Your cat is descended from the African wildcat, a truly solitary species. However, today's cats are no longer defined as solitary. Yes, the species as a whole is capable of living a solitary life, but cats are also capable of living in feline colonies or in a multispecies home. For the most part, they form strong relationships with us and potentially other species they live with, such as dogs. This does not mean that every cat is capable of living in these situations, but it does highlight how cats have adapted their social behaviour to thrive in the environment they find themselves in.

It was around ten thousand years ago, in the Middle East, that the domestication process began. Here, humans began creating settlements and building grain stores to feed the community. These grain stores attracted a steady supply of rodents, and, of course, cats soon followed. Not only did they hit the jackpot in terms of finding a reliable source of food, they inadvertently did humans a favour by protecting the grain. Their skill at keeping the rodent population under control was hugely appreciated, and so cats were encouraged to stay nearby and they took advantage of the available shelter. This sparked a change in the social behaviour of cats.

Cats began to spend more time around people, to stay closer to their food source – the rodents. The individuals that felt most comfortable with humans were more likely to nest and birth their kittens in closer proximity to the settlements. As a result, these kittens had the opportunity to get used to humans at a younger age, helping to drive domestication. These domesticated felines travelled the globe on ships and other vessels, keeping rodent populations on board under control.

The exact point at which the cat turns from mouser to companion can only be speculated on. Archaeologists have discovered feline remains buried alongside humans, and tombs decorated with artistic depictions of cats being worshipped as gods.

While the process of domestication brought cats and people together, it brought cats into closer proximity to each other too, and they were now competing for prey. This would have undoubtedly led to tension at first, but generally cats became more tolerant of each other, and the ancestors of the solitary African wildcat found they were able to live in harmonious groups.

Despite this, domestication hasn't much changed the cat as a species. We encourage cats into our lives for a quality they already had – avid hunter – rather than needing to selectively breed them for this trait. Isn't it ironic that now this is the behaviour we struggle with the most, with cats persecuted for hunting by those wanting to protect wildlife?

The process of domestication has been quite unintentional on both sides. Some will argue that cats are only semi-domesticated as we don't control 100 per cent of their breeding and domestic cats are still able to mate with non-domestic cats – for example, the African wildcat. They do not work for us or have any desire to please us. Yet it continues to be a relationship that benefits us both; we provide a home, food and social interaction, and they provide us with companionship. You really do have a little wild animal in your home.

2

The Sensory Cat

A cat's senses are incredible, but they are totally different to our own. The world they experience is not the same world we are seeing, hearing and feeling. It's hard to appreciate this when we live our lives so close to them, but your cat's physiology is that of a super-effective hunter whose senses are primed to aid their natural hunting abilities and their survival.

I love to sit quietly and just watch cats being cats. When you take the time to do this, and really pay attention to their behaviour, you begin to notice how their senses have developed and how they process the information around them. Watching their ears swivel independently as they try to pinpoint the location of a sound, or seeing how their claws remain sheathed during play but are out during hunting, is a fascinating experience. Understanding how they interpret the world gives an insight into the ways the environment impacts on their behaviour, and allows you to tune in to what it is they need in their home to flourish.

EYES AND EYESIGHT

Your cat's eyes are large in comparison to the size of her head, almost as big as human eyes, giving them their cute appearance. They help her hunt, so are adapted to seeing well in low light; perfect for hunting in those twilight hours when her prey is active. No wonder she is perfectly happy zooming around you in the early hours of the morning. This is down to the make-up of the rods and cones inside the eye and a pupil with the capability of opening to almost the size of the front of the eye so as to take in as much light as possible. In bright light, the pupil can shrink down to a thin slit to help protect the retina.

Cats are short-sighted (remember this when playing with her or handing her a treat) and not so good with colour, mainly seeing in blues and yellows and not so much in red. All those colourful cat toys are made to appeal to us, not our cats! Colour is largely irrelevant for a cat, it is movement that is important, and they are very sensitive to anything moving to help them detect nearby prey.

Have you noticed your cat's eyes glowing in the dark? This is due to a layer at the back of her eye called the tapetum lucidum that acts as a mirror and bounces light back out, giving them a glowing appearance. It is one of the reasons cats have been so revered throughout history.

EARS AND HEARING

Hearing is vital for effective hunting and a cat can hear much quieter noises than we can, such as a mouse rustling in the grass. This means we need to be aware of the louder noises in our home, such as the whirring of the washing machine or raised voices, as these will be much louder for her than they will for you. She can also hear a much higher frequency than we can, so can hear the ultrasonic sounds of prey animals. It is interesting that she can also hear low-frequency sounds too, so she is also able to hear and respond to your voice.

The shape of the ears helps to amplify sounds and each ear can rotate independently of each other to help them locate where the sound is coming from. It always makes me smile when I call Sparx and he doesn't turn around but graces me with his attention from only one ear!

NOSE AND SMELL

Smell is much more important for your cat than it is for us, as she uses it when hunting, investigating new objects, checking food before eating and in communication, especially around her territory. Be aware that she may be upset by strong smells, such as air fresheners or strong perfumes, as she has a more sensitive sense of smell than we do.

As well as smelling using her nose, your cat has an additional organ used for detecting and analysing scent and any additional feline pheromones that may be present, particularly in urine marks or facial scent marks from other cats. This is called the vomeronasal or Jacobson's organ and is located in the roof of a cat's mouth, connected to both her nose and mouth. When using the vomeronasal organ, a cat will perform the flehmen response: opening her mouth and intently drawing the scent in using her tongue. She may do this from a few seconds to over a minute, and, when she looks up, you may catch her 'flehmen face' – open-mouthed with her bottom teeth exposed. My brother and I used to quietly get each other's attention when we noticed our cat Lily was investigating a scent and would wait for her to look back at us with her cute, funny face even though, at the time, we had no idea then why she was doing it.

MOUTH AND TASTE

A cat's mouth is primed for hunting, with her canine teeth designed for swift killing of her prey and molars and pre-molars for shearing and chewing meat. And her tongue is covered in little keratin barbs called papillae which are not just for sandpaper kisses but are ideal for ripping meat from bones when eating her prey.

Cats do not have such a complex sense of taste as we do, and they cannot detect anything sweet though they can detect umami, a savoury or meaty taste.

WHISKERS

Cat's whiskers are fascinating. They are long, stiff hairs found mainly around the muzzle (around twelve on each side), but also above the eyes and on the back of the front legs. They are usually black or white and sometimes a cat will have a mixture of the two – I love seeing a cat that has a single black whisker in among lots of white ones. But whiskers are more than just cute, they are essential sensory aids. You may be surprised to hear they help your cat to hunt. Since her eyesight is poor close-up, once she's grabbed the prey, her whiskers take over, moving forward to touch the animal to help detect movement and guide her bite to exactly the right place.

They also help her to navigate her environment, as whiskers can detect air currents, to help gauge where objects are while moving through a room. Although whiskers do not contain nerve endings, they are embedded three times deeper into the skin than fur so should never be pulled out or cut.

TAIL

The tail is used for balance when traversing high places like fence panels or mantelpieces. A cat will adjust the position of her tail to keep her from toppling down. And should she fall, it will help adjust her balance and right herself so she lands on her feet.

PAWS AND CLAWS

Cat's paws contain glands that leave scent marks behind on the things she scratches. She sweats through her paws too; you may notice she leaves tiny sweaty paw prints on the vet's table if she's worried about being there.

Her claws remain sheathed when she is relaxed, and she can choose to extend them when needed. This allows her to engage in boisterous play behaviours with littermates and other friendly cats without hurting them, but the claws will come out in an instant if needed to defend herself.

FUR/COAT

A cat's coat is normally made up of three types of fur – down fur, awn hair and guard hair – though the exact make-up will depend on the breed. Down fur is a layer of short, soft hairs that help regulate temperature. Breeds such as the Cornish Rex have only down hair. Awn hair makes up most of the visible fur and is responsible for giving your cat her coat colour. It also helps to keep her warm. Guard hairs are longer and coarser than awn hair and help keep the body dry as well as warm. These are the hairs that stand on end along her back or on her tail when she is fearful.

3

Communication

Cats are notoriously difficult animals to read and understand, which is one of the reasons people who don't know cats very well, might not like them very much. They don't understand the significance of a slow blink or a little head bop, the way us cat people do. However, when you take the time to watch and learn from them, their body language and behaviour becomes a lot easier to read, and it helps us understand what they need from us to flourish.

Interpreting feline body language and understanding what they are trying to communicate is essential when I work with clients. I have worked with many aggressive cats over the past thirteen years, and this is one situation where accurately interpreting their body language is integral to my safety and the safety of the cat's person.

Many years ago I worked with a cat who had severely attacked an adult who was visiting her home. The adult was trying to play with the cat using a toy and had, without thinking, trapped him on the stairs that led to a closed door. The cat accidentally caught her hand with his claw during the game and the person had cried out in pain.

This particular cat was sensitive to loud noises and became fearful. At this moment, his body language changed and he was giving very clear signals that he was no longer comfortable. His body went from loose and bouncy to tense and rigid, crouching down and pulling away from her. His tail went from gently tapping every now and again during the game to being held low and tucked under. He began hissing and then growling before he was silent. This cat was essentially screaming at the person to back off, but she didn't listen to him and wanted to continue playing. He had no means of escape and flew at her leg, grabbing hold and biting down, causing significant injuries with his teeth and claws that warranted an immediate trip to the accident and emergency department. If she had only listened to him and moved away, she would have saved herself these injuries and helped the cat too, who was now fearful of people in general and attacking in many more situations.

When I met him, he showed the same behaviours towards me, so his carer and I both immediately knew he was not comfortable, and I knew to keep my distance to avoid an attack. I sat on the floor so as not to intimidate him and avoided making eye contact and he did not attack me. We knew we had to take things very slowly to help him learn to trust people again and thankfully he got there, but understanding the early warning signs he was communicating was an essential part of overcoming the problem and was necessary for the rest of his life.

But understanding your cat is not just about avoiding these distressing situations. It's about connecting with each other on a new level where you truly know how they are feeling. You know what your cat looks like when they are happy and when they are enjoying your company and it allows you to bond with them that much more closely. Take the time to learn to read your cat, open those channels of communication and make sure no one knows them better than you do.

BODY LANGUAGE AND BEHAVIOUR (VISUAL SIGNALLING)

The things a cat does allow us to understand how he is feeling. Every part of his body will be telling you something, so it is important to take in the whole picture rather than individual parts, and to be mindful of the context when trying to determine how your cat is feeling at any given moment.

Eyes

The shape of a cat's eyes are very telling in terms of how friendly they are feeling towards you. A slow blink from a calm and relaxed cat is a friendly signal. When a cat is giving you a hard stare (looking directly at you, unblinking), he's wary or threatened and you should move away. A cat that keeps its eyes squinted, regardless of how light or dark it is, may be in pain.

Their pupils can indicate how they are feeling too; they don't just react to light. Huge, dilated pupils in daylight indicate they are scared (which tends to be obvious as they will often be trying to escape from something), whereas cats feeling confident will have more natural, relaxed, thinner pupils.

Ears

Ear position is a little more difficult to decipher as they move so much in response to sound, however, they are a good area to keep an eye on when your cat is experiencing a strong negative emotion. For example, if he is very scared of you and cannot escape, his ears will be pulled right down, almost flat to his head, and he will be pulling away from you. The ears of frustrated cats are often turned downwards, almost to make a straight line from one ear tip to another. Cats in pain can hold their ears slightly turned so you can see part of the back of the ear from the front, so keep an eye on this if your cat holds his ears this way all the time. Ideally, his normal ear position will be upright and forward, and responsive to sound.

Tail

Many of us love dogs as well as cats, but some people have a better understanding of dog behaviour than cat behaviour. And a wagging tail is probably the most obvious sign of a happy dog (although it's much more complicated than that). For cats, the opposite is true and, generally, a moving tail is not a sign of a happy cat. A cat that is feeling scared or defensive may hold their tail tucked low and under the body.

When you're stroking your cat, a small twitching near the tip of the tail can be the first indication of when he has had enough. If you don't stop, you might notice the tail begins to move more intensely, thrashing from side to side (that's if they haven't jumped away by now), which is a sign they are becoming very unhappy. I would not recommend trying to stroke a cat whose tail is thrashing – it is unlikely to end well.

Experts are divided on the meaning of a vibrating tail. This is often displayed when a cat is urine-marking, but will also be shown at other times, which I have heard referred to as 'fake spraying'. Some experts say this is a friendly behaviour, others say anxious, so which is it? My feeling is that it's a sign of high arousal – which could be positive or negative. It could be the excitement they feel when you walk through the door, and they know food and attention will soon follow. But I've noticed they will also do this when feeling conflicted. For example, when introducing my dog, Bucky, to Fig and Sparx, I noticed Sparx's tail quivering when Bucky was getting a bit too close. Though Bucky's intentions were friendly, he was making Sparx uncomfortable by sniffing round his ears and neck – Bucky has no sense of personal space!

The thing I love to see the most is a cat trotting towards me with an upright tail with a small curve at the top. It's a very clear, super-friendly greeting that cats display towards us and towards other animals. This is the equivalent of a dog with a waggy tail, so you should be equally happy when your cat approaches you this way.

Fur and skin

When a cat is scared, you may see their fur stand up on end on their tail, in what is often affectionately called 'toilet-brush tail', or on their back so they look like a traditional Halloween cat. The proper term for this is piloerection – and it's not a sign of a happy cat.

The cat's skin may ripple too, particularly on their lower back, which often indicates something is irritating them.

Whiskers

When your cat is relaxed and friendly, his whiskers will protrude from the sides of the muzzle. If he becomes fearful, they can be pulled back out of the way of any potential aggression that may be on the cards, whereas if he is instigating aggression (rather than reacting defensively), the whiskers can be slightly pointed forward. They are also pushed forward during hunting to help provide more information about his prey.

The direction your cat is looking

This may sound odd, but the direction a cat is looking can give us a lot of information. If you approach a cat and hold out your hand towards him, does he look towards you and approach, or does he look the other way? If he looks the other way, it is unlikely he wants to interact with you.

This often happens with cats that want to be on your lap but don't want to be stroked. They will actively approach and plant themselves on you but look away when you try to touch their head. The same is true for posture. If he is leaning away from you, trying to look as small as possible, he is not comfortable in this situation. Whereas if he is upright and confident, he is much more open to interaction.

Paws

Watch what your cat is doing with his paws. If he swipes at you, it's obvious that he wants you to move away; this will be done with claws if he is really serious or without claws if it's more of a warning. Remember, cats are stimulated by movement, so if you move quickly around them, you may trigger a swipe without them really knowing what they are swiping at.

Hopefully, you have seen your cat kneading, also described as 'making biscuits' or 'baking bread'. This is an affectionate behaviour often performed when looking to settle down and get comfortable. They learn this during the time spent with their mother, as kneading her stomach stimulates the milk flow as they feed. If his pinprick claws are hurting you (we've all been there), grab a blanket for your lap before the kneading starts. You really don't want to discourage this behaviour, it's a nice one, and, besides (if your home is anything like mine), once he's settled, you're excused from making tea until he's up again!

Another challenging behaviour is your cat pawing at you because he wants something. This is commonly food, but

can be your attention. This usually starts as an accidental behaviour, but cats are opportunistic, so reaching out
towards food or an object they are interested in is a natural
behaviour. Be warned though: once he has been rewarded
with the food or item, he will try it over and over. And if you
refuse, frustration builds – and here is where the claws come
out, not because he is trying to hurt you, but because he is
trying harder to get the food. Prevention is better than cure
in this situation, so take care not to reward attention-seeking
behaviour from the outset. If you already have this problem,
ensure he has a very consistent feeding routine, where food is
given on your terms rather than in response to his behaviour.
You can help break the habit of pawing for food by redirect-
ing his attention to something else, such as a toy, or moving
yourself away from him for a short period.

Teeth

Biting is a behaviour used during hunting (or play), or as an
act of aggression intended to make the target move away.
Your cat may give you a warning bite, where he touches
your skin with his teeth but does not entirely bite down.

Drooling

Some cats will drool when they are happy. It is not clear
why some cats do this and others don't, but it is nothing
to worry about unless it is out of character or happening
constantly.

VOCALISATIONS

Cats have a wide range of vocal sounds that can be used to communicate with people and other cats. You can tell a lot about how your cat is feeling from their vocalisations. The reassuring sound of a cat purring quietly next to you as you sleep is bliss. Whereas the unmistakable sound of cats fighting at night, out in the street, is enough to have us leaping out of bed and running to the window to make sure it's not our cats involved in the fray.

Meow

Adult cats rarely meow to one another, but it is a sound that is commonly heard between a mother and her kittens. If a kitten becomes separated from the nest, he will call, and his mother will respond. It is interesting that cats commonly meow to people as, just like the mother, we respond to it (with our attention and other positive inter-actions) and the meowing quickly becomes reinforced, happening more frequently. How many of us answer our cats when they meow? Almost everybody!

Purr

Your cat's purr is the loveliest sound. Sparx sleeps on my pillow and each night I lightly press my ear against his side and listen to the quiet rumblings that are almost undetectable when I take my ear away. It is commonly believed that cats purr when they are happy or content, and for the most part this is true. However, there is a lot more to purring that we are only now beginning to understand.

Kittens first purr while they are still with their mother and will purr FURIOUSLY as they feed, while their mother purrs back in response. This is an ideal form of communication, reassuring the mother that her kittens are feeding well, and reassuring the kittens that their mother is here and they are safe. They can also purr with their mouths closed or full, which is ideal for purring while feeding.

Your cat may purr when they want something from you. This purr will sound different to the slow, rhythmic vibrations and will be higher pitched, more urgent and combined with other behaviours such as leading you to the kitchen or trying to initiate physical contact from you. This is called a solicitation purr.

Cats can also purr when they are in pain and those in the veterinary profession will be no stranger to this experience. Those with serious injuries or illness may be feeling very unwell but will continue to gently purr. It has been found that purring of a particular frequency promotes pain relief, so may be an attempt at self-healing and coping with painful situations.

Chirruping or trilling

This is usually a friendly greeting towards a person, cat or another animal.

Hissing

When your cat does this, he will pull his lips back over his teeth and make a hissing sound.

This is an aggressive vocalisation with an intention to get the target to move away. It is a warning that physical aggression may follow and can be directed at people, other cats or other species. It may also be directed at an object such as a blanket that smells of another cat. It is often performed when cats are scared or something has startled them, and is very common in aggressive interactions between two cats or between a cat and another species, such as a human or dog.

Spitting

This is a similar behaviour to hissing, but is much shorter in duration and makes more of a click noise from the back of their throat. It is a sign of aggression.

Growling

This is a low, long-drawn-out noise to indicate he would like the target to move away. He may do this prior to an aggressive interaction or as a warning while eating or holding food/prey in his mouth. This can also apply to toys; you may find your cat holds a toy in his mouth and growls if anyone comes near.

Yowling or howling

Another long-drawn-out vocalisation, usually heard ahead of a fight or between bouts of fighting. If your cat makes this sound around you, move away from him quickly.

Caterwaul

A very intense, high-pitched, almost screaming noise made by cats during fighting, when they are very scared, or when they are in acute pain. It is often over very quickly as usually the cat will try to escape as quickly as possible.

Chattering/chittering

This appears to be the only form of vocal communication that is not directed at another cat or person. It is the sound your cat performs when he is looking at birds or another potential target, but is unable to catch them. It happens commonly through a window but can happen when birds are out of reach. It is not clear why cats chitter, but the most likely explanation is that it's an expression of frustration.

SCENT-MARKING

This is the secret language of cats: a method of communication almost completely undetectable by us, but of utmost importance to your cat and the other cats around you. Even as tiny kittens, they rely on the scent of their mother and the rest of the litter to locate the nest and their mother's milk supply. As an adult, your cat uses scent-marking to leave information around his environment to help it feel familiar and for other cats to investigate.

There are several ways cats scent-mark and he (and she – both males and females can scent-mark, even urine spray) does this to deposit pheromones from his scent glands (located at various points on his body) that contain unique information about him, such as his health, age and sexual status, as well as when he left the mark. These pheromones help mark out territory, help attract a mate and help to establish a bonded social group. Being surrounded by their own familiar scent is also reassuring, especially if there are potential threats in or around the environment.

Cats will investigate scent marks using their vomeronasal organ, using the flehmen response to pick up this information from other cats and learn about the other cats in the area. They can then make decisions based on this information, such as whether to go outside and when. Here are the ways in which scent-marking takes place.

Facial-marking

Cats have numerous scent glands on their face including on their cheeks, above their eyes and on their lips and chin. This is why you will notice him rubbing his face on prominent areas of your home and, if you're lucky, he may even rub his head against your hand or face too. My Fig is the best for this.

Facial-marking is a really positive behaviour when performed inside your home. It shows he is confident, content and happy. Take care not to wipe down the surfaces on which he has facial-marked as these are important signals that help him feel safe in his home. If he doesn't feel safe, you may find he 'ups his game' and moves on to urine-marking.

Body-rubbing and tail-wrapping

Cats also have scent glands at the base of the tail and along the length of the tail too. This is why they are inclined to rub against your legs with their face, body and tail while you feed them: they are marking you. The same behaviour is sometimes seen between free-roaming cats that live happily in groups; sometimes members of the group will trot alongside one another with their bodies pressed together and their tails intertwined. This is so lovely to see, but in my experience it's very rare to find this behaviour displayed between pet cats in the same household.

Scratching

Scent glands on the bottom of a cat's paws allow him to deposit pheromones on the surfaces he scratches. This is why he may prefer to scratch the arm of a sofa in the middle of the lounge (a prominent location in an important part of his territory) instead of the cat tree you have placed in a spare room that he rarely visits.

Urine-marking and middening

Cats have scent glands around the anus that deposit pheromones into their urine or faeces. It is totally normal for cats to mark this way in the outside world, however, it is not so normal inside their home. Most cats are confident enough to rely on facial-marking, body-rubbing and scratching inside, which allows them to keep their home clean. So it is a sign that something is wrong if they use this form of marking indoors.

4

Understanding Breeds

The popularity of the cat as a companion animal has seen an increase in the diversity of the species, and people have recently begun to intentionally breed cats for a specific trait or quality rather than choosing a moggy with mixed or unknown ancestry. Unlike dogs, which were historically bred to fulfil specific functions, cats have generally been bred for purely aesthetic reasons, such as the way they look.

This means there is less variation in the behaviour of cat breeds than you find among dogs. With dogs, you must give due consideration to the type of dog you are looking to bring into your home, as it could be fundamental to how well they settle in and whether they can fit in with your lifestyle. You need to think about how much energy they will have, how many walks they might need, how easy they are to train and what they have been bred to do (chase, herd, retrieve, for example) as this will impact on the life you share with your dog.

With cats, you still need to be aware of the common traits of a particular breed, but those traits will have less impact on the life the two of you share. Finding a cat whose temperament and personality fit with your home and lifestyle is more important than which breed you choose. That being said, you should not choose a breed without doing your homework on that particular breed's special needs and characteristics, especially with breeds that traditionally develop extreme features.

BREEDING EXTREME FEATURES

Humans love novelty. Anything different to the norm piques our interest and their popularity soars. But deliberately breeding cats with extreme features can be detrimental to their welfare. For example, brachycephalic cats like the Persian typically have a flat face and shortened airways and can suffer associated health issues. Other examples of extreme features include the Sphynx, which has very little fur, and the Munchkin, with its shortened legs.

I got Sparx as a kitten back in 2009. He is a Cornish Rex with short, curly fur and I loved the idea of my cat having something different to a regular cat and, honestly, didn't give much thought to how this would impact his life. Fourteen years older and wiser in the ways of cat behaviour and welfare, and I can recognise how important this is to consider. He doesn't like going outside unless it is really warm because his fur is short and his poky, curly little whiskers won't provide him with the same experience as Fig's long and flexible ones. He is at higher risk of some health conditions, but thankfully he isn't showing any signs of these.

You may think these are small concerns, but to spare our amazing cats from unnecessary suffering we need to be mindful of the impact of breeding extreme characteristics. I am not totally against these newer breeds, but responsible breeding that sees welfare rather than looks as paramount is essential to the long-term health of this beautiful species.

PHYSICAL HEALTH

As cats are bred for looks, some common physical health problems associated with particular breeds have been accidentally bred into them. For example, hypertrophic cardiomyopathy – a type of heart disease – is a health concern for the Persian, British Shorthair, Sphynx, Maine Coon and Ragdoll, among others.

Burmese cats are prone to orofacial pain syndrome – a painful condition that causes them to scratch at their mouth and tongue. I have seen a fair few of these cats for behavioural treatment and it is very distressing to witness. The increased risk of such health conditions in these breeds and others is not intentional but is an unfortunate inheritance we need to be aware of. Any responsible breeder will be aiming to breed these conditions out where possible, through appropriate testing and only breeding from healthy individuals.

Other types of health issues are a direct result of selective breeding. For example, the Persian has been bred for shorter skull bones to give them their flat-faced appearance. The fallout of this is they can have difficulty breathing as the airway develops abnormally.

Another example is the Scottish Fold, a breed that has a genetic mutation affecting the development of cartilage.

This gives them their characteristic folded ears, but it can lead to bone and cartilage abnormalities throughout their bodies, resulting in painful joints and severe arthritis. Although these problems with the Scottish Fold are widely recognised, potential owners who fall in love with their cute appearance are liable to overlook the potential health issues. A quick Google search will bring up tons of kittens looking for homes, but do your homework and be aware of the potential health conditions of your new best friend. Choose a breed without such severe health concerns or, at the very least, ensure the breeder is responsible and has invested in genetic testing to minimise the risk and promote a healthier breed. There is more information on finding a suitable breeder later on in this book.

MENTAL HEALTH AND BEHAVIOURAL IMPLICATIONS

As well as ensuring our cats are physically healthy it's important to consider their mental and behavioural health. The ability to perform natural feline behaviours is something that is paramount to mental well-being, and, for some breeds, this ability is compromised because of some of their features.

Coat length

The length of a cat's coat can have a significant impact on how that cat behaves. I have already mentioned my cat,

Sparx, with his thin, short coat. The problems he experiences are even more extreme for Sphynx cats, who only have a very thin layer of down hair and often no whiskers at all. As a result, they are not suited to spending much time outside due to the risk of sunburn and their inability to stay warm in cooler temperatures.

On the other hand, some long-haired breeds such as the Ragdoll can struggle to maintain their coat through grooming, so it quickly becomes matted. A Maine Coon owner recently turned to me for help because he was struggling to get all her knots out as she hated being brushed. If you choose a long-haired breed, you need to commit to regular grooming. Once mats begin to form, brushing will be painful for the cat and her resistance will make grooming an ordeal for both of you.

Communication

The physical characteristics of some breeds can compromise their ability to communicate with other cats. For example, the Japanese Bobtail or any breed with a stunted or totally missing tail will not be able to indicate when they are feeling irritated by swishing it, nor can they approach with the classic 'tail up', friendly posture. Similarly, those with no or shorter fur are unable to display piloerection, which could impact on how they are perceived by another cat. Likewise, those with distorted ear shapes may not be able to show as clear signalling as a cat with the traditional ear shape.

Temperament

For the most part, reputable cat breeders do very well with breeding for great temperaments (there is more on breed temperaments in a later chapter). Plenty of breeds are described as highly intelligent, sociable, playful and affectionate, such as Bengals, Siamese and Rex breeds. Others, like the Ragdoll and Persian, are described as being friendly, gentle and playful. It is difficult to find a breed with a bad word said against their temperament, although the breeders writing the descriptions are usually very passionate about their breed!

This is not to say you can't find these desirable personality traits in your non-pedigree moggies, but many (if not most) non-pedigree cats are 'accidental litters' which have come about because the owner hasn't neutered their cat. In these cases, the owner will have little or no control over which male their cat mates with. To complicate matters, a single litter of kittens can be sired by different fathers if the female mates with more than one male in close succession.

The males in these cases could potentially be feral or strays that are not overly sociable, friendly or playful – and we know kittens can inherit some behavioural traits from their father, even if they never meet him. So, a non-pedigree temperament can be more variable than a pedigree.

You should also bear in mind that positive traits associated with certain breeds can be challenging. For example, Siamese are very sociable, but they are also very vocal, often 'talking' to their owners for attention. Their intelligent nature means they pick up bad habits very quickly and before you know it, your Siamese is meowing at you day and night, which some people love but others will struggle with.

Hybrids

This is another area where we need to be careful with selective breeding. A hybrid is the result of mating a domestic cat with a wild cat. The most common examples are Bengals (domestic cat mated with an Asian leopard cat) and Savannahs (domestic cat mated with a serval). It is clear that we are in dangerous territory here, in that the early descendants of these pairings may inherit more of the wild side than the domestic side, and the behaviour of subsequent generations can still be challenging.

However, these breeds do tend to get a bad rep, being unjustly labelled as aggressive. Bengals are indeed high-energy and intelligent animals, so they need to be housed in an environment that provides the right outlets for this energy. The same goes for Savannahs; they are not aggressive per se, but they may not adapt as well to human lifestyles as other breeds. Many of these animals are kept inside due to their tendency to roam and their territorial behaviours with other cats, but this means their behaviour is amplified in a smaller environment and tensions may rise with other cats – or you could become the target of misdirected play. Acquiring appropriate veterinary care can be a challenge too as if even the friendliest Savannah does not want to go into the cat carrier, attempting to manoeuvre them inside can be dangerous.

PART TWO

Finding the Right Cat and Settling Them In

5

The Right Cat for You

Adding a new cat to your family is an exciting time and an experience we want to go as smoothly as possible. The general misconception of cats being a low-maintenance animal leads some of us to think any cat will be suited to any household when, in fact, not every cat fits with every situation and a mismatch can lead to problems for both you and your cat. A cat that is not happy inside your home may use its access to the outdoors and 'vote with their feet', moving out to take up residence in a more welcoming home nearby.

Set yourself up for success from the start by choosing the right cat or kitten for your lifestyle. Think about your life now and how this is likely to change over the coming years. Your cat needs to be able to settle into your current lifestyle and adapt to any changes as they happen.

IS IT THE RIGHT TIME?

Before bringing your first cat home, or adding another cat to your family, give careful thought to whether this is the right time. With the advances in veterinary care and the increase in cats being kept exclusively indoors, cats are living longer than ever. Of course, this is a wonderful thing but it means the decision to add a cat to your family can be one that affects your life for the next twenty years. With cats, more than any other species, it is very common to hear that a friend of a friend has a litter of kittens they are looking to find homes for, so you may be tempted to agree to take one without giving it as much thought as you might with a puppy or an exotic pet. Here are some things to consider:

FINANCES AND OTHER CONSIDERATIONS

Keeping a cat is not cheap. You have the initial cost of purchasing or adopting your kitten or cat (although your next cat may just turn up at your house and invite themselves in), which can vary wildly depending on the breed. You should expect to pay something for your kitten or cat; you want them to have come from a good home (or a reputable rescue centre) where they haven't been exposed to unsavoury or even high-risk situations. (And if you find yourself with a litter and are tempted to advertise the kittens as 'free to a good home', be wary of scammers who will sell the kittens on for whatever they can get, regardless of what kind of home they go to). There is more on this issue in chapter 7.

The next expense will be providing your new cat or kitten with a complete set of the things they need: food bowls, water sources, cat trees, litter trays, cat carrier, toys, etc.

Food is obviously an ongoing expense. Ideally you want to avoid providing your cat with the very cheapest food, as some may lack key components of a nutritionally balanced diet. Another essential is cat litter, as they absolutely need to have a safe place to pee and poo when they are feeling vulnerable.

If you can, I would recommend insuring your cat. I understand it is another outgoing that you can potentially avoid, but it is heartbreaking to find yourself unable to pay for the veterinary care your cat needs. Many insurance companies now cover the fee to see a behaviourist, which is a huge relief for my clients.

Time

Once your kitten or cat arrives home, they are going to take time to settle in. This is critical when dealing with a rescue cat who has been mistreated, or if you already have a cat and are looking to introduce a new one. With a rescue cat, they may choose to hide from you for a long while before finding their confidence. Have you got the time and patience to let this happen?

When introducing a second cat to your home, they will need to be kept separate from your other cat initially. A slow introduction should then follow that can take many weeks or even months before they can be left unsupervised. If your cats don't get along, you need to have enough space to effectively create two separate territories inside your home permanently. Can you accommodate these separate areas in your home? Do you have the time and patience to carefully integrate a new cat?

43

Are you home enough? If you are out at work all day, it isn't fair to adopt a cat that you'll only be with during the evenings, overnight and nothing more, particularly if it's an indoor cat. Outdoorsy cats with the freedom to come and go usually cope better with being left alone as they have plenty to keep them occupied outside. If you know you are going to be leaving a kitten or cat at home alone for long periods, opt for two kittens or an adult bonded pair to keep each other company.

Finding the perfect addition

In order to find the cat that has the best chance of slotting into your home and living a happy and healthy life with you, think about the challenges your home poses and consider whether it will suit the cat's needs.

Environmental requirements

For example, do you have children or other animals in your home? Is your home a busy and noisy environment or a calm and quiet place? Do you have lots of visitors? Are you planning renovations? Or moving house sometime in the future? Will your cat be confined indoors or free to go outside? What is this outdoor space like? Are there lots of hazards or sources of stress out there? Are you open to rehoming a cat with a medical condition? Or one with a difficult history who may need additional time to settle in? Or who has high grooming requirements?

All these things need to be considered when finding the right cat for you. Ideally, you need a cat that has had good experiences in these situations already, so they can more readily adapt to your home and lifestyle.

Grooming requirements

Don't underestimate the challenge of grooming cats. Long-haired cats are beautiful, but they are liable to need help maintaining their coat in hard-to-reach areas like under their armpits and along the lower part of their flanks, especially as they get older. This is something you need to be proactive about, brushing them as part of a routine to keep long fur in good condition. If you don't, and you wait until the fur becomes matted and unkempt before doing anything about it, you will have a much bigger problem on your hands.

Brushing feels a lot nicer for the cat when the fur is mat-free, so they will be more tolerant and, hopefully, enjoy the experience. Knots and mats make brushing painful, and you will have to keep going until the knots are out, which is often more than your cat can stand. Some mats won't be able to be brushed out and you will need to use a groomer, which can be a stressful experience for the cat and expensive for you. If things get too bad, you could ask your vet to shave the knots off, which they may need to do under sedation – and that comes with its own risks. It is much easier all round to keep on top of grooming from the start.

BREED CHOICE

If you are looking for a particular breed of cat rather than a moggy, there are some additional considerations to take into account. Moggies make great pets and there is so much variation in their character and temperament that you don't know what you're going to get; all you can do is judge whether this individual cat is right for you based on their socialisation, experiences and genetics (which will be covered later). With breeds, you need to be prepared for some inherited tendencies that may influence whether this is the right cat for you.

Take Burmese, for example. In my experience, the Burmese is a very high-maintenance cat. They are super-sociable, which makes them entertaining and rewarding animals to live with, but also quite demanding. They are not suited to being left alone for long periods and are one of the most common breeds I work with for behaviour problems. And they take this to the next level too; a friend's Burmese once sprayed urine into her parents' bowl of porridge. But he also adorably burrowed into her dad's jumper and poked his head out the top so they could watch TV together.

Bengals are a breed I often see too, but they are easily labelled as aggressive which I don't think is fair. Yes, they need stimulation because they are intelligent and agile cats with a territorial nature. If you don't engage them with fun and stimulating activities, or provide them with a fun and stimulating environment, problems can surface, such as misdirected play – and this hurts because they are often bigger and more muscular than your average moggy. I have seen this plenty of times, but with the right outlets and the right management, Bengals can make lovely pets. If you have a busy life and limited space, a breed such as this, that needs a high amount of input to keep them happy, may not be your best choice.

Siamese cats are intelligent, sociable breeds so can be very vocal. Some are prone to pica – chewing or ingesting foreign objects such as wool or plastic. Some people love this about their Siamese cats, but it is something you need to be prepared for if you decide to take one on.

Sphynx cats and Rex cats have a reputation for being mischievous – and I quite agree! Extreme breeding aside, I have never met a Sphynx or Rex I didn't like, and their mischievous nature is a product of high intelligence and a need for stimulation.

ADULT OR KITTEN?

Kittens are a popular choice as this is when cats are at their cutest. A common perception is that they don't need much input at that age – they will already be litter trained, so none of the midnight toilet trips you would expect with a puppy. The biggest challenge is they need a LOT of play-time, especially if you have a single kitten. They are particularly popular with children as they are fun to play with, and most confident and friendly kittens will enjoy playful interactions with sensible children. Their claws and teeth are not overly painful at a very young age either. However, the tricky age is around nine to ten months, when they are still very playful but much bigger, and their claws and teeth can do a lot more damage.

That said, there are many benefits to choosing an adult rescue cat, especially if she is going to be your only cat. She will be past her challenging adolescent stage and (as long as she is friendly) will settle in quickly, ready to be your new best friend.

The average lifespan for a cat is around thirteen to fourteen years, though plenty live into their twenties. If you are not looking for such a long-term commitment, adopting an older cat can work for you both. The downside is you are unlikely to have much information on their history, and they may have behavioural problems (or even health problems). But don't let this put you off. For many cats, a change of environment can be enough to overcome problem behaviours.

If you are an older person yourself, or have an older person living with you, a kitten can cause problems. Bites and scratches can be painful and there is a high risk of infection.

WHEN YOU DON'T GET A CHOICE

The independent nature of the cat means that often your new cat will find you. Strays will wander in and claim your home as their own, given half a chance. Just keep in mind, as much as we want to take good care of every cat, the one that decides to move in may not be a good match for your home. Stay objective and give it time to see whether this cat fits into your home or if you can find better help for this cat by contacting a reputable rescue centre.

6

Factors That Shape Your Cat

Now we have dealt with the cat as a species, it's time to understand what makes your individual cat unique.

PARENTS

Your cat's mother and father have more influence on her development than you may at first realise.

Genetics

We can see the role of genetics by looking at the behaviour of the sire. In most cases, he would not even meet the kittens once they have been born (unless the breeder has both mother and father and lets them interact), so any inherited characteristics from him are down to genetics alone. It has been found that 'boldness' is a trait inherited from the father, which affects confidence levels. Try to ensure your kitten has been sired by a friendly and confident father by asking questions about his temperament.

Social learning

The mother plays more of a role than just genetic inheritance as she brings up the kittens and they learn a great deal from her behaviour before leaving the litter for their for ever homes. If she is wary of people and displays aggression when they approach, the kittens will learn to be afraid of people and will show a similar response. This is why, if she is aggressive, it is important to handle kittens away from their mother once they are old enough to feel comfortable being apart from her. If she is friendly towards people, this will be of huge benefit to the kittens as they are more likely to feel comfortable around people and show friendly behaviours themselves.

I saw a good example of this last year. I met two of the cutest Siamese kittens who were bundles of fun and happiness until their owner got out a wand toy. They continued to play but would hiss at the toy during the game. When I asked about this, I was told their mother had shown this exact behaviour too. There is likely to be more to unpick here, but it was an interesting observation of social learning.

She will also help her kittens to regulate their emotions by creating situations where the kittens show a particular emotional response. For example, feeding and sleeping in the safety of the nest will be comforting and reassuring, helping the kitten feel content. However, during weaning, the mother will deny them access to her milk by sitting in such a way as to prevent the kittens reaching the teats or simply moving out of their reach. This will instil feelings of frustration which the kittens work through and can then cope better with as adults.

Ideally, you should aim for your kitten to be born from a calm and friendly mother and stay with her until they are twelve weeks old.

Prenatal stress

The stress the mother experiences while she is pregnant can impact the behaviour of the kittens once they are born (for more on this, see John Bradshaw's *The Behaviour of the Domestic Cat*) and there is a biological reason for this. If kittens are born into an environment where the mother has experienced stress, such as being chased by a predator, because of prenatal stress, the kittens will be more reactive to challenging situations which increases their chance of survival by making them better equipped to escape predators.

The difficulty is that once you home these kittens to calm and safe households, they will retain this increased reactivity and may experience stress at the smallest thing, such as meeting new people or a loud noise.

Keep this in mind: if your kitten's mother was feral, a stray or lived in poor conditions while pregnant, your kitten may not be as confident and well-rounded as you might like.

EXPERIENCES

Between two and eight weeks of age is a vital period in your kitten's development where the experiences they have will shape their behaviour as adult cats and will determine how well they can cope with the potential challenges of life with humans. During this time, it is essential they are well socialised (helped to feel comfortable with people and other animals), habituated (helped to feel comfortable with their environment) and appropriately handled. If this does not happen, your new addition is going to struggle to cope with life around you and in your home. As most kittens go off to their for ever homes at twelve weeks (sometimes as young as eight weeks), the entirety of this important period is spent with the kitten's breeder (be it a professional breeder, hobby breeder or accidental breeder), in rescue or, in the case of strays or ferals, potentially living freely. This means once your kitten is with you, the window has passed and their socialisation is totally out of your hands, so you must make sure you spend time finding the right kitten for you, rather than feeling you can shape a cat to fit in with your lifestyle. There is more on finding a breeder later on; for now, let's look at the experiences they should have between two and eight weeks of age.

Socialisation

Socialisation focuses on the social development of the kittens and involves helping them learn that people and other animals are friendly and can be trusted. So, you need to be sure your chosen kitten or cat has been appropriately and carefully exposed to a wide range of people (with various physical attributes) and, ideally, any animals your cat will be living with, before eight weeks of age. For example, if you live with children or children visit regularly, it's best if your cat has encountered children of around a similar age and had a positive experience with them. This is so they learn that children are friendly and nothing to be afraid of; they can then generalise this to include all children, not just the ones they have met.

Care needs to be taken to ensure all interactions are positive and pleasant. Negative experiences with people or other pets can lead to long-term changes in your cat's temperament – and not for the better. For example, if a kitten has been mistreated by a human, it could come away from that experience thinking that people cannot be trusted. To prevent this, breeders need to ensure that people take care around the kittens. Not every experience needs to be hugely rewarding, it is more about appropriate exposure to help them understand that living with people is normal and OK.

My family and I recently had the pleasure of helping to socialise some kittens for my local cat rescue in their foster home. My children are nine, seven and four and my husband is tall with a beard, so as a package we were pretty perfect to help the kittens learn that different types of people are friendly. The hard part was making sure the two five-week-old kittens we were meeting were having a nice time, as it could have been overwhelming for them being around so many strangers. In fact, it went perfectly.

My children sat on the floor and were sensible and calm, waiting for the kittens to approach them and managing to contain their excitement when the kittens began climbing up onto their legs. Once they became more confident, we chatted to them and to each other, to expose them to regular conversation. Gradually, my children began to move around a little while playing with them. If only more breeders and rescues would be so proactive in calling in help with socialisation if they need it.

Habituation

This focuses on helping kittens feel comfortable with the world around them and involves them learning to ignore things in the environment that are not important. For example, kittens growing up in the breeder's home will experience the noise of the TV, vacuum cleaner, kitchen appliances, toast popping up, toilet flushing, the phone ringing, somebody knocking at the door, the post falling through the letter box, I could go on and on. This is an ideal environment as the breeder doesn't have to put any effort or time into exposing the kittens to this. As long as the kittens have access to the main living areas of the home and are generally happy and healthy kittens in every other way, they will be learning all about environmental stimuli as they go.

Again, care must be taken around the kittens to ensure this exposure to everyday stimuli is appropriate. For example, if somebody drops a saucepan on the kitchen floor and it makes a huge clattering noise, the kittens are likely to be startled and may potentially become fearful of loud noises. They should be exposed to these noises at a level they are comfortable with; any noisy activities should be done in another room, so they can hear it but are not worried by it.

If kittens are not able to habituate to a normal human environment, they risk feeling anxious in their home, so ask the breeder whether the kittens have been reared in the home or if they have been confined to a shed or outbuilding.

Handling

Handling is another important experience kittens require between two and eight weeks of age. Many cats and kittens don't enjoy being picked up or handled too much, but such is human nature that undoubtedly every pet cat will have been picked up at least once in their life. So, helping them to feel comfortable with physical interactions with humans is essential. Research has shown that kittens require at least forty minutes of gentle handling per day, but split into short handling sessions rather than all in one go. This should be with a range of different people to help with the socialisation and help them accept being handled by more than one on person.

Individuals should go gently by frequently stroking the kittens around the head and neck area, as this is usually well accepted. They should also occasionally stroke along their back, tail, legs and paws to get them used to this feeling. Gently picking them up is important too, giving lots of breaks and incorporating interactions you know they enjoy, such as playing with toys to prevent them becoming too overwhelmed and to make it a positive experience.

As well as helping them cope with well-meaning, over-enthusiastic interactions, it is also important to prepare the kittens for veterinary examinations and treatment. For example, they need to feel comfortable with gentle restraint, looking in their ears and eyes, opening their mouth, projecting their claws, grooming with a soft brush and parting the fur on the back of their neck in preparation for preventative parasite treatment. Your vet will thank you for it, and it will be a huge relief for you when you take your cat to the vet in the future and he is an absolute dream rather than that cat that comes with a warning.

It is not just the experiences they have during their sensitive period that are important. Any negative experiences they encounter at any age can cause a change in the way they feel, much more than with positive experiences. For example, if your cat is well socialised to dogs and is comfortable around them but is one day attacked by a dog, this distressing event may be enough for them to be fearful and uncomfortable around dogs for life. So although the socialisation window is closed, it is still essential to be mindful of avoiding potentially negative experiences.

Similarly, it is not impossible for cats to learn that something that used to be scary is actually OK. A good example is feral cats. Generally, feral cats are fearful of people as they have not had many (or any) positive experiences with people, especially not during the two-to-eight-week window. However, many people are able to gain the trust of a feral cat over time with sensitive interactions, which is lovely to see. What is usually happening here is the feral cat learns this person will not hurt them and usually brings nice things (food). But it does not mean they are now socialised to people, and this trust is not usually granted to anyone else other than the person who has put in the time. This is not true socialisation, socialisation is generalised to 'people', not just 'person'. There is more about living with feral cats later as this is a very controversial area of cat welfare.

This whole process of socialisation, habituation and handling is about preparing cats for an emotionally stable life where they can confidently deal with the challenges of everyday life with humans and are prepared for and resilient to the stressful events that will undoubtedly happen as they share up to fifteen or even twenty years with us. Yes, you might accidentally step on their tail one day (and naturally hate yourself for it), but because of their solid socialisation and the trust you have built since then, they can cope with it and their relationship with you won't break down. Or they are resilient to fireworks going off outside as it's just another random noise in their surroundings.

7

Finding the Right Cat

When looking for a kitten or an adult cat, a rescue centre would be the perfect first stop to enquire about a new addition. There are always cats in need of homes and your perfect companion may be there waiting for you already.

By the time a kitten is ready to come home with you, whether from a breeder or from a rescue, the all-important window for socialisation will have closed. This means you are putting all your trust in the kitten's breeder or rescue centre to ensure it has had appropriate experiences throughout this time. You must do your homework on this; ask the breeder or rescue questions and if their answers leave you in any doubt, walk away and wait for the right match to come along.

Finding the right match for your family and your home is crucial to set you up for the relationship you are looking for with your cat – whatever that may be. Some people want an affectionate lap cat, others want more of an independent being who does their own thing and checks in on their own terms. If you find the wrong cat, it can spell disappointment and frustration for you that your cat is not doing what you expect of them, and the cat will struggle to settle if you are asking for something from them that they are not happy to give.

I have seen these situations where no one is happy. I recently had a lengthy phone conversation with an elderly lady who wanted a calm and affectionate older cat to sit on her lap in the evenings and she was upset that the cat she had just rehomed was not at all interested in being a lap cat and kept herself to herself. This is not something that could be easily changed; the cat simply wasn't interested in that sort of physical interaction. On the flip side, I once visited a lady who thought she had taken in a feral cat from a rescue to live in her shed. She was happy to provide him with food, water and a warm comfortable place to sleep (these sorts of homes are massively needed, so she was doing something amazing!), but it turned out her 'feral' didn't want to sleep in the shed, preferring the indoors. She was upset when he kept sneaking in through open doors and windows and she would frequently come home to find him asleep on her bed. This was not what she'd signed up for, so she was asking me how to get him to be happy staying outside. As you can imagine, this didn't really seem appropriate, so he found a new home with a person who was happy to offer a comfortable life inside, while her shed became home to a truly feral individual.

Sometimes cats are just in the wrong environment and do not flourish/cannot cope. If this is the case, behaviour problems can develop and often cannot be undone without significant changes to the environment or a complete change of home. It's so much better to take the time to find the right cat (kitten or adult) from the start. Granted, it's not all about socialisation (later experiences, the environment and other sources of stress come into it too), but you stand a far better chance of building a happy life together if your cat has been set up to thrive in your home environment.

FINDING THE RIGHT BREEDER

If you are buying a kitten from a breeder (be it a professional, hobby or accidental breeder) it is essential you do your research and gather as much information as possible on the breeder, the cats, the kittens' experiences and the environment. Remember, you are putting all your trust in the breeder to make sure they have raised your kitten as a good match for you, so ask a LOT of questions.

If you have a cat already, you may find this section explains some of the behaviours he or she displays. If you are concerned your cat has not come from a good breeder, don't worry. Throughout this book you will learn how to address any challenging or unwanted behaviours your cat displays that stem from the approach of their breeder.

Information about the breeder

If you are choosing a pedigree breed, the breeder should be registered with an appropriate organisation, be paying for health checks and have experience of and passion for the breed. They should be able to tell you what to expect from the breed as a whole and should show enthusiasm for their personalities and behaviour. Be wary of breeders that work with more than one type of breed (or species) as it may be more of a money-making exercise rather than a specific desire to pass on their cat's genes and add to the population of their favourite breed.

If you are looking for a moggy, this is more likely to be an accidental litter or a more informal mating than with pedigrees, where a free-roaming, un-neutered cat has mated without their owner knowing. In this case, the cat's owner won't be so knowledgeable on a specific breed, but should still show enthusiasm for the kittens and feel their cat has an ideal temperament and is passing on desired traits in her kittens. Any breeder should show knowledge and understanding of each kitten and should be able to tell you about the behaviour and temperament of each to help you find a good match for your home.

Ask the breeder how the kittens have been socialised. This should be an active process. Check how many people they have met and if they align with your circumstances. For example, have they met men, women and children? What people and animals live in the home? Have additional people been visiting and how did the kittens behave? Have they been gently handled routinely? It is the responsibility of the breeder to put in the time and effort to ensure this has been done appropriately. The same is true for noise, and there are many sound effects online they can use to help the kittens become familiar to thunderstorms, fireworks, babies crying, etc., all played at a low level so as not to overwhelm or startle them. The breeder owes it to you and the kittens to do a good job of preparing the kittens for life with people (as well as physically caring for them), or they should not be breeding at all. They should be happy for you to interact with the kittens and handle them too.

Do you feel you have a connection with this breeder? Do you feel happy with them and the way they have been communicating with you by sending updates and pictures? Do they seem interested in how the kittens are growing? Go with your gut and walk away if you are not happy or unsure. They should care about the homes their kittens are going to, so should have plenty of questions for you, too.

The breeder should be open to you being fully involved with the kittens where possible. They should be happy for you to visit their home (multiple times if necessary) to get to know the kittens and their mother. This will be ideal for you as you can see the environment and the behaviour of the animals in the home firsthand (more on this below). If they don't want you visiting, or arrange to hand over the kitten anywhere but at their home, it could indicate the kittens (or their mother) are displaying behaviour problems (such as aggression or toileting issues) they don't want you to see. I was called to see a young kitten who was peeing on her owner's bed, despite having suitable litter trays. The kitten's breeder had arranged to meet her at their local vet's to hand the kitten over, which my client agreed to without thinking too much about it. I found this odd as it would take more effort for the breeder to take the kitten out than have her collected from home. When we looked back at the photographs my client had been sent, we noticed that in all of them, the kittens were confined to a large bed and there were no pictures of them in rest of the home. We suspected the kittens may have been peeing on the bed then, not something you would be open to letting anybody see.

Ideally, you should be able to collect them at around twelve weeks of age, but some people do allow kittens to leave their mothers at eight weeks, which is not advisable. It should never be younger than that, as they may not be completely weaned and sufficiently developed emotionally. Try not to get talked into taking them early, as exciting as this would be.

Finally, they absolutely must be charging a fee for the kittens. That is not to say they must be charging a fortune and churning out kittens to make money, of course that is not what we are looking for. But asking for a fee shows they are helping to ensure their kittens go to responsible owners. Advertising as 'free to good home' is not OK. These breeders often care little about where they go and just want rid of them. There is a risk these kittens will be picked up by someone without good intentions and the kittens may find themselves in a dangerous situation. It is perfectly reasonable to charge a fee for this reason and to recoup some of the costs of caring for a litter of kittens for three months.

Accidental breeders

By this I mean those who have let their female cat outside before she has been neutered. This could be a genuine mistake or oversight – she may have escaped or perhaps the owner didn't realise how easy it is for them to fall pregnant, but often it is due to owners who consider cats to be low maintenance and so are not giving them the care they need by neutering before letting them out. I once met a client who went to collect her kitten from a local resident. A young cat had had kittens, one of which had later fallen pregnant, and the mother was pregnant a second time too. The owner of these cats had not meant for this to happen and was trying to care for them all before finding them homes, but the kittens and their mothers were suffering as a result. There really is no excuse for not spaying, and this is discussed later in this book.

That being said, ethics aside, accidental litters in family homes where the cats are well looked after actually make pretty good family pets. They are usually fully exposed to the comings and goings of a regular home. They are often busy households and the kittens get used to the hustle and bustle of everyday life.

Information about the kitten's parents

Some breeders keep a stud cat for breeding purposes, as well as the queen (mother). The good side of this is that you can ask all about the temperament of the father and may even get to meet him if you are lucky and can judge for yourself how friendly he is. The downside is it is difficult to keep a stud and a queen together and many studs end up in an enclosure away from the home. This is because they are more likely to urine-mark and may try to mate with the queen at an inappropriate time. This can mean they receive less interaction with people and their welfare may be compromised if they are frustrated with confinement. With more casual breeders where the queen has mated outside without the owner knowing at the time, it is very likely the owner won't even know what colour the father was, let alone the temperament. An added complication here is one litter can have a mix of kittens fathered by different cats.

In most cases, unless kittens are being reared by hand, the queen should always be present when you are visiting and collecting your kitten. This will help you judge her character, and watch how she behaves around the kittens. If she displays any aggression towards you when you come too close, this is not a good sign. The kittens will learn to be fearful of people from observing her, which may continue into adulthood. Keep this in mind for other behaviour problems too, like toileting on surfaces such as soft furnishings or carpet, and aggression towards other animals in the home.

It is wise to ask for more information about the queen, such as how old she is. Kittens can fall pregnant from four months of age, and this is just not OK. At that age her body will not have fully matured, and growing and sustaining kittens so young can impact on her development. She may be more likely to reject the kittens. A breeder who allows this does not have their cat's best interests at heart, which could reflect on the kittens.

The cat should be at least eighteen months to two years of age and, ideally, not younger than five years of age. Although technically cats can have multiple litters per year, this is not in the mother's best interest as she will need time to recover in between pregnancies and enjoy life without the constant responsibility of rearing kittens.

If she is very young or has had multiple litters in the past, it may indicate the breeder is prioritising money over the well-being of their cat and I would recommend steering clear of this situation.

If you are buying from a professional breeder, the owners of the stud and queen should be aware of the common health concerns of the breed and will take steps such as genetic testing to ensure the parents are healthy and they are maintaining the overall health of the breed. With moggies, the gene pool is so varied health checking isn't a necessity (but never hurts!), but you should ask if both cats are generally healthy or are suffering from any health conditions.

Information about the kittens

Firstly, it's important to ensure the kittens are healthy and the breeder has taken the first steps in preventative healthcare. For example, are the kitten's ears, eyes, nose and back end clean? There should be no concerns with the kitten's mobility or their appetite and there should be no signs of parasites (such as fleas or flea dirt) on the kittens, the parents or in and around the home. The breeder should have started the kittens' vaccination process and should not be allowing the kittens to go outside this young. They should also be feeding the kittens on a commercial diet specifically formulated for kittens. I have come across breeders in the past who have found it difficult to stop their adult cats and kittens eating each other's food, and so have fed all the cats on adult food as it is cheaper than kitten food. The nutritional value of kitten food is appropriate to aid the physical development of the kittens, so it's problematic if the breeder can't find a work around to give the kittens the food they need.

Ask how many cats the breeder has in their home. Multiple litters of kittens may indicate they're operating a kitten farm, especially if the house is not being lived in. It may also indicate the kittens are being bred in a cat hoarding situation; in these cases, the breeder means well, but there are too many cats to properly look after. In both cases, it is unlikely the kittens would have received enough attention or care and the risk of disease and aggressive interactions with other cats is therefore higher. On the flip side, kittens growing up without siblings often miss out on learning appropriate cat behaviour and communication from other kittens and this may affect their relationships with other cats later on.

The behaviour of the kittens is important too. Yes, there will be variations between the kittens' temperaments and this is lovely to see, but there are some behaviours that should be considered a red flag. For example, the kittens should not show any aggression towards you or towards each other. This can be difficult to pinpoint, as their play looks so aggressive with kittens biting each other's faces and bunny-kicking each other furiously, so look out for aggressive vocalisations such as hissing or growling; this shouldn't be happening at such a young age unless there is something for them to truly fear. If they are hiding excessively and do not appear for the duration of your visit there, this is not normal behaviour. If this is the case, you are going to have a very challenging cat on your hands that you will hopefully be able to bond with over time, but the likelihood is they will always be fearful of new people and try to hide. You are looking for confident kittens that approach you on their own initiative and are not startled by you moving around or talking to them.

They should be totally litter trained before they leave the litter so if you notice any signs of toileting issues such as a rogue pee or poo in the wrong place, they may not have very good toileting habits. Any kitten that has been trained to pee on newspaper, for example, will learn newspaper is a thing to be peed on and is at risk of doing this her whole life. What are the queen's toileting habits? Kittens learn by watching her, so if they see her peeing on a blanket rather than in the trays, they may follow suit.

If the breeder has other adult cats in the home, observe how they interact with the kittens or ask the breeder for some video footage. If the adult cat is hostile towards the kittens, this could be setting them up for poor social relationships in the future. Every interaction needs to be positive at this stage.

Finally, ask how the kittens have been socialised and compare this to your specific living arrangements. Have they met other cats? Have they met a friendly dog of the same size as yours? Have they lived with or met children of the same age as yours? If so, ask about the nature of the relationship. It's not just about being exposed to these people and animals, it needs to be done in a controlled and positive way so the kitten feels good about being around them. In some cases (for example with dogs), no exposure at all during their time in their litter can be preferable to a single interaction that ended badly, causing the kitten to feel uncomfortable around dogs for ever.

Information about the environment

Ask the breeder (or see for yourself) where the kittens are being kept throughout their time with the breeder. Ideally, you are looking for them to have access to the main living areas of the home – living room and kitchen, with plenty of safe spaces such as cardboard boxes, cat beds, the nest site the queen chose, etc. This will help to ensure your kitten has been appropriately exposed to the noise of a regular household and will settle into your home without any issues.

If you have young children at home or hope to have children during your cat's lifetime, find a breeder who has children too. This is not just so the children can handle and interact with the kittens; living with children also means the environment is going to be quite different to that of a home without children. There may be loud, unpredictable noises, it might be a busy environment with lots of feet passing by. If your cat has been bred in a quiet household, it is difficult for any breeder to replicate this in an appropriate way, so look for a cat that has been raised in a house with sensible children, so they are completely comfortable with everything that comes with it.

Kittens that are housed outside in an outhouse or kennel, in crates, or even in a single bedroom without any access to the rest of the home, may miss out on essential learning experiences during the sensitive period of two to eight weeks. Stay clear. Many years ago my husband and I went to view a litter of huskies as I was observing them for a university project (and of course my husband wanted to play with husky puppies). When we arrived, the puppies were housed in a small pen in a spare room downstairs, and I happened to notice a litter of kittens confined to a small dog crate on a table top in the corner of the room. This is absolutely not OK and when I asked about it, the breeder explained the kittens were caged just while we were visiting to keep the kittens away from the puppies, but it did not seem to add up. The house was also very dirty, the breeder did not seem to show much love or care for her puppies or kittens and it felt like the product of very irresponsible breeding – for money rather than for the love of bringing healthy cats and dogs into the world.

FINDING THE RIGHT RESCUE CAT

If you are choosing a kitten from a rescue centre, follow the advice above in terms of the development of the kittens and the behaviour of the parents. It is even more important to ask the rescue staff how the kittens have been socialised. Unless they are with a fosterer, they are likely to have spent their lives in the rescue so they are unlikely to have the opportunity to get used to the commotion of a human household and may not have the chance to meet many people, depending on the rescue's policy. Sound effects may be used to help familiarise the kitten with everyday sounds and ideally the staff will encourage plenty of people to head in and meet them.

If you are looking to rehome an adult cat, it is essential

you ask for as much information as possible about their history as it can be crucial to determining if they are a good match for you, how easily they will settle down in your home and understanding why they perform a certain behaviour problem if one presents itself later down the line. All too often the rescue will have told my client that they have no knowledge of the cat's history at all. This is probably true as so many are picked up as strays, but it's so disappointing and happens so much more frequently than with any other animals due to a cat's tendency to roam.

If you are ever in a position where you are surrendering your cat to a rescue centre, it is important to be honest with the staff as the more information you can provide, the easier it will be to find them the right home and avoid your cat bouncing between the rescue centre and potential homes before finding the one that works. If your cat has shown aggressive behaviour, it would be wise to rehome this cat to a place without children or older people living there, as they are vulnerable if bitten or scratched. If they have been peeing in places where they shouldn't, yes, it may take longer to find a person willing to take them in with this issue, but once they have found a home, the new owner can take steps to avoid this issue happening again.

One thing to bear in mind is that the cat's behaviour in rescue will not be totally reflective of their behaviour at home. Don't ignore the ones hiding at the back; some really struggle in a rescue environment but once you get them home and give them time to settle, you will probably find they show a complete transformation.

TAKING ON A STRAY CAT

Such is the nature of cats that one may appear one day at your door, move in and refuse to leave. I have many clients who describe this as 'my cat found me', which is lovely if the stray is genuinely a cat in need (and not a free spirit enjoying life as a stray, including taking up residence in several different houses from time to time).

Taking on a cat is a big commitment and it's important to make sure your cat is a good fit for your home. Not to say you should never take in a stray, but there is a lot to think about, and it is OK to say no to the stray who wants to move in and is looking worse for wear.

That's not to say you can't help them. If you suspect they are stray (they may be unkept, skinny and hungry), and you are able to get them into a cat carrier, you can ask your vet or local rescue centre to scan them for a chip and reunite them with their owners.

If you do decide to take them on, you may notice additional challenges that are not so common in cats who haven't lived freely outside. For example, they may be more likely to show aggression to any other cats you have, as most free-living cats have had altercations with other cats in their past. They can often be very food motivated, raiding cupboards for food and scarfing their meals in a few seconds because food is often scarce when you are fending for yourself. Finally, your previously stray cat may have trouble adapting to an indoor lifestyle as he has been so used to having the freedom to go where he likes.

TAKING ON A FERAL CAT

Feral cat means just that: feral. They are cats that have had no (or very little) positive interactions with people during their early development. They are born outside, away from people and prefer to stay this way. So often I hear owners refer to their aggressive or stray cats as feral, but when the cat is in the right mood, they are affectionate, calm and relaxed in a human household. These cats are often wayward strays rather than genuine ferals. I visited a lady who had taken in a feral kitten that was hanging out in her garden and was now showing aggression. I turned up expecting to be met with a wild animal, only to find the cutest and most friendly kitten who was overwhelmed and uncomfortable being picked up. This was not a feral kitten at all, and I had an awful feeling this lady had essentially stolen someone's pet kitten. Sadly, they were not microchipped and, despite asking her neighbours and on social media, she could not find the original owner.

Feral cats are usually born to feral mothers who experience a high level of stress while pregnant. By stress I mean potential lack of food and shelter, interactions with predators, aggressive interactions with other cats, etc. Here is where she will experience stressful situations during pregnancy that are liable to affect the development of the kittens, preparing them for a life of hardship rather than a life on your sofa. As a result, they can show more challenging behaviours, such as increased reactivity in situations that other cats can cope with.

Although it seems like attempting to rehome feral cats is the right thing to do, once they are over four months of age, this is seldom the best option for feral cats. For starters, they are difficult to home. Very few people are looking for a cat that wants nothing to do with them and that they can never touch, so these cats end up in rescue centres for long periods of time waiting for the dream farmhouse or stables to live in.

If they do find a home, they can experience high levels of stress from stimuli their non-feral counterparts may be totally fine with, such as raised voices or the toast popping up. For feral cats, the indoor life means living with their nerves permanently on edge, and they will be far happier back outside. If you manage to successfully gain the trust of a feral cat (and that takes a LOT of time and patience), all of your hard work will be unravelled once they need veterinary intervention. Many ferals cannot be treated without sedation. And that's assuming you can manage to get them into the carrier at home. You risk undoing all your good work and you'll both end up being miserable. The most appropriate approach to helping feral cats is to leave them alone and take care of them from afar by providing food, shelter away from your house and appropriate veterinary care (if possible), through the Trap, Neuter, Return (TNR) schemes.

8

Helping Your Cat Settle In

Bringing your new feline family member home is a very exciting time for all the family. But it also comes with a sense of uncertainty and often anxiety. This little being will hopefully be your new companion for many years to come, but you may find yourself wondering if you've done the right thing? You might worry about providing the type of home your cat needs and may even wonder if he or she is going to like you, particularly if they're of a more nervous temperament. The pressure can feel too much and you might question whether this is the right cat for you after all. Or whether a cat is even the right species for you. These initial worries are completely normal, especially if you have never lived with a cat before or haven't for a long while. You should feel reassured that you are here, taking the time to understand all the things your cat wishes you knew, so I have no doubt you can give your cat an incredible home, even if it means making changes here and there to accommodate her specific needs.

Helping her to settle into your home quickly means you can start the wonderful process of getting to know her and bonding with her. Preparation is key, whether you are bringing home a kitten or an adult cat. You need to plan ahead to help her transition from the breeder, rescue centre or previous home to your home go as smoothly as possible.

Firstly, you need to buy all the essential things your cat will need before she comes home. This will include:

- A least one litter tray.
- A good supply of cat litter. Ideally, the same type she has been using when living with the breeder or in rescue.
- At least one scratching outlet such as a post or cardboard scratcher.
- Separate bowls for food and water.
- A supply of age-appropriate cat food. Again, keeping to the same type and brand that she is used to will help her settle in. If you are so inclined, you can look to gradually change this later on once she is settled.
- Plenty of different types of toys. Kittens will need a lot of object play after spending twelve weeks playing with their littermates, especially if you have only adopted one kitten rather than two.
- Numerous different types of beds – including ones she can hide inside, and climb on top of.

If your new addition is a kitten, it is useful to initially buy smaller items to encourage her to use them. For example, kittens may struggle to climb into a high-sided litter tray or may feel overwhelmed by a gigantic cat tree. Smaller ones can help set up good habits for their use, but be sure to replace these objects as she gets older and larger. You will also need a suitable, secure cat carrier to transport your cat or kittens to your home safely. An open carrier should become a permanent part of her territory, offering a safe place to hide if she suddenly feels overwhelmed.

Kitten proofing/household hazards

Protecting your kitten from hazards in your home is essential. A mischievous kitten will undoubtedly be climbing up the curtains the moment you turn your back, and she'll find all sorts of ways of getting in trouble and danger if you don't take precautions. (Some of these are relevant for older cats too.)

- Block access to any small gaps or holes – the last thing you want is your kitten getting stuck behind the washing machine and having to dismantle your kitchen to get her out.
- Tidy away loose cables, electrical cords or anything else she can get tangled in. Chewing cables is a common problem which can result in electric shock and younger cats are at risk of becoming tangled up. Place fishing-rod-type toys out of her reach when you have finished playing with them.
- Kittens can choke on small objects or ingest foreign objects such as rubber bands, and she will want to bite or chew on them as part of her natural curiosity and enthusiasm for exploring all parts of her new home.

- Be mindful of keeping toxic or dangerous foods out of her reach such as chicken or fish bones that can get stuck in her throat or insides. As a child I came home from school one day to find my cat Lily had ripped into my Christmas advent calendar. Thankfully, we caught her before she had eaten any chocolate, but it was a close call and just shows how they like to keep us on our toes.

- Certain flowers and plants can be poisonous and need to be kept out of reach of cats, or out of the home and garden completely. Every part of the lily is severely toxic – the stem, leaves, pollen and flower – and ingesting a small amount from chewing the leaves or licking pollen off their fur can lead to severe kidney failure which can be fatal. Even drinking the water from the vase can be deadly. There are numerous other poisonous plants, so make sure you do your homework on flowers before bringing any home. We generally avoid flowers altogether – it was a sad day when I had to donate my wedding bouquet, but it wasn't worth the risk as Sparx would make a beeline for a chew on the leaves and stems.

- Many chemicals used in the home and garden are hazardous for cats. Antifreeze is a common source of poisoning as it seems to be somewhat palatable, and cats have been known to lick spills from the car, puddled on the ground. Ingesting just a small amount of antifreeze can be fatal, so spills need to be appropriately cleaned, and quickly. All other chemicals, such as cleaning products, should be stored away safely and surfaces allowed to dry before your cat can walk on them.

- Medication prescribed for humans should never be given to cats as paracetamol and other pharmaceuticals can be harmful and potentially fatal.

Avoiding these hazards can be a bit of a shock to the system at first, but before long it will become second nature and you will easily be able to keep your cat safe within your home.

Once they are home

Allocate a room in your home for your cat to go to as her safe base. If you have a busy home, this should be away from the hubbub of everyday life so she can have a calm environment to settle into. I find bedrooms to be perfect for this; as well as spending time up there with her when she first arrives, you can sleep in there overnight – and being around a sleeping person will help her get familiar with you and the room without any pressure to actually interact, or any risk of you inadvertently making her uncomfortable by paying her too much attention too soon. This is much easier to do if you do not already have a cat and don't have to figure out the logistics of who is going to go where, not to mention the challenge of introducing the two of them – don't worry, this is covered in later pages.

Once she is safely home with you, she will need time to settle in. If you have a sociable, well-rounded and people-focused individual, you may find she isn't interested in hiding; instead she is keen to explore, happy to approach you and ready to play. This is an ideal scenario, however, even the most sociable cats and kittens still need time to decompress and take stock of their new surroundings before getting to know you and your family and exploring the rest of the home. As difficult as you may find it, it will pay off to give her that time; let her explore when she is ready, and allow her to approach you and interact in her own time.

Finally, no doubt there will be plenty of people ready to meet your new cat or kitten and you might be super-excited to show her off. Nevertheless, it pays to wait a few days before having anybody over to visit, and keep her to yourself for a little while. Kittens will usually have come out of their shell by this point and it will be a much more satisfying visit for your kitten and your friends if she has already started to grow in confidence.

With rescue cats, much will depend on their temperament and previous experiences. Some may relish the attention and be ready to engage with anyone and everyone who crosses the threshold; others will be hesitant or even avoidant, and will not be ready to interact with anyone else for a long while.

RESCUE CATS

Rescue cats bring different challenges and may have additional requirements to help them adjust to life in their new home, particularly if you have a very fearful cat. She will be looking for somewhere to hide, so provide plenty of hiding opportunities that are safe and easily accessible so she doesn't panic and disappear behind the sofa for a week.

This can be so upsetting to see – if only we could tell her that she is safe and can trust you.

The key to helping her settle is not to put any pressure on her to come out and let her do this in her own time. Pulling her out from a hiding place or blocking off any potential area to hide will remove any feelings of control she has and will leave her feeling vulnerable, scared and overwhelmed – the exact opposite of how we want her to feel. Let her hide! Encourage her out with treats (and toys if she is younger) and treat her like an invisible cat when she makes those first tentative steps out into the open. It's tempting to jump for joy – or at least say hello to her – but you risk her disappearing right back to her hiding place. Her confidence will come in time and will give you an opportunity to bond. To help with this process, it is useful to know as much of your new cat's history as possible, to anticipate how she is going to feel towards you and a new environment. From here, you can begin to slowly get to know her and understand her specific needs, her boundaries and her comfort zones. Earning the trust of a rescue cat is a long process, but it's so rewarding knowing how much you have helped her and getting to enjoy each other's company – it is well worth the time and dedication.

PART THREE

What Your Cat Wants You to Know

9

What Your Cat Wants You to Know about Neutering

If you are wondering if you should have your cat neutered, the short answer is yes, absolutely. Unless you are a professional breeder and are looking to breed from a healthy, friendly cat, it is better all round to go ahead with the procedure as early as four months of age. This is the age from which your tiny kitten can fall pregnant and kittens having kittens is the saddest thing. Male kittens can reach sexual maturity this early too and, as you will see, it leads to huge problems if you let your male cat outside without him being neutered first, even if the resulting kittens won't be your problem.

Cats reproduce very quickly, and one female can be responsible for the birth of thousands of kittens if her offspring are not neutered either. Anybody working in cat rescue centres will tell you that neutering your cats is essential. These centres are crammed with cats and kittens looking for homes. Finding space for cats in need and suitable homes for those already in their care undoubtedly feels like a never-ending challenge. As soon as one cat successfully moves on to their new for ever home, another one is waiting to take their place. We often hear 'Adopt, Don't Shop!' which is an important way of helping cats needing homes. However, neutering before they have an opportunity to contribute to the kitten population can be an even bigger help. Most rescues will neuter cats before they leave the shelter, so if you are set on bringing home a kitten from a breeder, or have taken in a rogue, entire stray, neutering should be one of the first things on your list to organise.

It is not just the growing population of cats that is the problem here. Entire cats (those that are not neutered), particularly males, are difficult animals to live with. With sex hormones at play, his priority will be finding a mate, not being your lap cat. If he can go outside, he will probably roam a lot further than his neutered neighbours, potentially crossing busy roads in search of mating opportunities. If he crosses paths with other males, he will have a reason to fight them – they are competition and therefore liable to be considered a threat. This means fights are common and so are the injuries and abscesses that come with them – it's a tough life being a tomcat. This can cause significant issues for other cats in the area who feel intimidated by entire cats encroaching on their territory. When he is home, it is unlikely to be for long, and if you try to keep him inside, there is a very good chance he will urine-mark, either to attract a mate or because he is frustrated with being confined. I will not see a client for urine-marking in the home if their cat is not yet neutered. It doesn't seem fair to try and stop it when it is a totally reasonable and expected behaviour – it comes with the territory, if you'll excuse the pun.

When I was younger we had Spooky, our beautiful tabby who birthed a litter of kittens. Naturally, I loved it, and begged and begged my dad to keep one of the kittens. Finally, he relented, and we kept Sammy – the cutest, fluffiest tabby you could have ever met. He was super-friendly – his socialisation must have been on point! – but once he was older, I remember it being a happy surprise to see him; he would turn up when it suited him for food and a comfortable place to sleep for a while before he was off again for days at a time. He was a massive, heavy-set cat; as friendly as he was with me and my family, there is no doubt he would have been a formidable competitor in a fight, and there were always scabs to be found under his fur. He loved human attention but his priority was not being my best friend. I do wonder what he would have been like if he was neutered as a kitten. He would undoubtedly have had an easier life.

Entire female cats do not pose as much of a challenge for their caregivers day to day, however, the behaviour of a female in heat can still be problematic. She may become super-affectionate, which isn't a bad thing for us, except when she begins calling in search of a mate. These are loud meows that happen a LOT and are very difficult to ignore. There will also be changes in her body language. She may roll around on her back more frequently and adopt a pre-senting posture where her back arches downwards, leaving her rear end up with tail held to one side, essentially in position for mating. Aside from this being very annoying, it is generally manageable, and you may feel that keep-ing her inside is a good alternative to neutering as she won't meet any potential mating partners and therefore cannot have kittens. But bear in mind how many litters are accidental, with cats escaping their home and returning pregnant – and they will have far more motivation to get outside than their neutered counterparts. Ovulation is triggered by the mating process itself, so there is no safe time to let her out when she cannot become pregnant. She may be in heat and open to being mated with, without you realising. Regardless, it is questionable whether it is ethical to allow her to go through this experience of coming into season while denying her any opportunity to actually go out and find a mate. The frustration she will experience will be significant.

The fact is that neutered cats generally live longer and there are real health risks to living a life as an entire cat. Birthing too many litters of kittens puts a huge strain on the queen, as does having kittens too young. She may reject the kittens as she prioritises her own health and development. Male cats can go on breeding for years, meaning they continue to roam and fight throughout their lives, struggling to keep up as they get older and are challenged by younger and healthier competitors.

You might be wondering if they are any positives to keeping your cat entire. In my opinion, there are none. It is not necessary for a cat to experience her first season; there are no welfare implications here that have been observed. It is not kinder to protect them from the operation when we then expect them to live as pet cats and not wild animals. Cats should not be used as a teaching tool for children to experience the miracle of life. I can see the benefit of sharing your home with four tiny newborn kittens for twelve weeks, but, honestly, the benefits to us nowhere near outweigh the potential consequences for the cats. The cost of the neutering procedure (which is more expensive for females than males) should be factored in before you bring your kitten or cat home. If you have an unneutered cat already and the expense is not something you can cover, there are charities that will help – showing just how important those in the welfare sector consider neutering to be. If you are breeding cats for the sole purpose of making money rather than passing on healthy, friendly genes, you should not be a cat owner at all.

Keeping the kitten population under control has wider implications too. If you are concerned about wildlife populations, as many are, neutering pet cats can help. Free-living cats have a bigger impact on wildlife than cats living in our homes, but pet cats and their offspring can quickly find themselves back in the wild population, hunting to survive. In only a couple of generations, kittens descended from pet cats can revert to feral individuals who will be living with minimal (or no) contact with people, breeding freely. TNR programmes can be put in place to help control the population of free-living cats. These programmes exist to keep the cat population under control and to protect the welfare of the cats no one is caring for, or those cared for by a group of local residents. If only we all played our part with neutering at the earliest opportunity, it would avoid a significant amount of suffering in the bigger picture. Cats are being persecuted for the declining wildlife population, so let's do what we can to help in the most ethical and welfare-friendly way.

10

What Your Cat Wants You to Know about Territory

Cats are naturally territorial animals and retain much of their territorial nature despite living happily in human households. This means how we set up our homes, gardens and other spaces really matters to them and can have a big influence on their behaviour and, ultimately, on their well-being.

THE TERRITORY OF FREE-LIVING CATS

Cats are a unique species in that many live freely in the UK without any (or little) input from people, whereas others are firmly home-loving cats. To help understand what your cat needs from their territory in your home, it can help to think about how free-living cats behave.

A cat's territory will naturally centre around essential resources: food, water and shelter. For free-living cats, this can mean plenty of hunting opportunities and shelter from the elements. I remember a feral colony of cats living in Longleat Forest Center Parcs and thinking it was the perfect place for a colony of cats, with the forest full of wildlife and the trees offering areas for shelter and nesting. Cats that are neither feral or living with people may choose to live on farms or in towns where they can source their food (either given by humans or foraged, and often supplemented by hunting) and shelter (making use of barns or anywhere they feel warm and safe from predators). This safe and familiar area becomes their core territory and the surrounding area in which they head off to explore for hunting or mating opportunities becomes their home range. Their core territory is defended from unfamiliar cats that are not in their social group, though it is common for the home range of different cats to overlap.

YOUR CAT'S TERRITORY

So how does this translate to your home and your cat? The inside of your home should become their core territory – the place they feel safe, where can relax and play and have a reliable source of food and water. Their core area may shrink to a single room or area if they don't feel safe throughout your entire home. Your cat may not be open to sharing their core territory with any other cats, which is why it is important to introduce a new cat slowly to ease them into the idea.

If your cat has access outside, this will become their home range. The size of the area they cover will depend on the individual and the surrounding environment, with some cats roaming a lot further than others. If you have a confident, active, outdoorsy cat, he might roam further than a more timid, placid and home-loving cat. If you live in an urban area, he may not roam as far as a cat living in a rural area with forests and fields to be explored. One thing is for sure, no cats concern themselves with human garden boundaries. To them, fences and brick walls are highways to access other gardens rather than barriers.

The number of threats in the outside environment will also impact on where your cat roams and how far he'll go. And these threats do not need to be genuine dangers, they can just be something he is worried about. For example, next door's dog may be friendly and pay no notice to your cat, but he may still give that garden a wide berth. As with free-living cats, his home range is likely to overlap with other cats in the area, but if the number of cats is too high, it can lead to conflict and may cause problems.

If you keep your cat entirely indoors, he will not have the opportunity to establish a home range outside of his core territory. When you think of how cats live if left to their own devices, it is amazing to think how well they adapt to living a totally indoor lifestyle. On the other hand, those with free access outside may well establish multiple core territories within their home range, heading into other houses and treating these as home. I have seen cats with more than one owner, each unaware of the other, and there is a whole internet phenomenon of 'my house, not my cat' where people come home to find an unfamiliar cat making themselves at home.

DEFINING/MARKING TERRITORY

A cat's territory is mostly defined through scent rather than by sight. However, the way in which they do this can change, depending on which part of the territory they are marking. Cats usually mark their core territory through various forms of scent-marking:

Facial rubbing

As mentioned earlier, cats have scent glands located in several areas of their face including their cheeks, chin and the area above their eyes. They will actively rub their cheeks or the corners of their mouths on prominent objects in their core territory, like the corner of the coffee table or a wooden door frame. Your cat might also do this on you, giving you a little head bunt as a sign of affection and social cohesion. They may do this in the home range surrounding their home too, but facial marks do not withstand the elements for long.

Sleeping and body-rubbing

Cats leave their scent behind wherever they have been sleeping and you may also see your cat rolling playfully around on their back, flipping from side to side. The places they sleep the most will become the places they feel most secure which is ideal for helping the inside spaces feel secure. Again, this sort of marking is too subtle to be very effective outside.

Scratching

The glands located in cats' paws leave their scent behind when they scratch on a surface. This is why cat trees become a very important part of a feline's territory inside the home, as well as items of furniture that are unmoving such as sofas, banister poles and even carpets. In their home range, they can scratch on trees, logs and fence posts to leave visual scratches as well as a scent mark.

Urine-marking

This involves spraying pee horizontally onto a vertical surface that can be investigated by other cats in the area and is the perfect form of long-distance communication. It allows them to leave messages for other cats in the area, and define their territory without ever needing to come face to face with them. Urine-marking allows them to avoid risking conflict with other cats and, as you will see in later pages, this is paramount to their well-being,

Middening

This is marking with poo and again tends to happen out-side the home. Usually poos are left in a very prominent area, such as right in the middle of your lawn (and it usually won't even be from your own cat). Again, pheromones are deposited into the poo, acting as an obvious 'I was here' mark for all to see.

This tendency to use subtle methods of scent-marking inside and more obvious methods outside works perfectly for keeping their home clean while meeting their need to establish and maintain a core territory and a home range. Of course, urine-marking does happen inside sometimes, and it is one of the more common behaviour problems I am asked to help with. There are many potential reasons for this, but it is usually a sign your cat feels threatened inside their home and the normal methods of marking inside are not reassuring enough. They need to up their marking game to satisfy themselves their core territory is a safe place. Threats include anything they find stressful such as other cats coming too close to the house (or even inside the house), or anything that changes the scent profile of the environment – renovations, redecorating or new furniture, for example.

SETTING UP YOUR CAT'S TERRITORY

One feature of your cat's territory that will be super important to her is the ability for her to comfortably spend time up high and off the ground. This is because she is both a predator and also a prey species, which significantly influences her behaviour. Being a solitary hunter, from an evolutionary perspective, she knows she cannot rely on another cat to provide food for her so sustaining even a small injury can risk her ability to hunt and, ultimately, her survival. Therefore, the inherent motivation to get off the ground is strong, so she can keep an eye on her territory from a safe place, and take hunting (or play!) opportunities when they present themselves.

I saw a classic example of this recently while I was out walking my dog, Bucky. He was off lead, and we were wandering down a wooded pathway that ran along the back of some residential gardens. I noticed a cat perched on top of one of the six-foot fences. She had spotted Bucky and was wide-eyed and staring at him, but instead of running away, she actually moved towards him from her safe spot up on the fence. She had a vantage point and felt confident enough to handle being so close to a large dog because she felt safe up there. This is the confidence we want to give to our cats inside the home when we set up their territory.

Provide plenty of opportunities for her to get up high, using cat furniture specifically designed for this as well as utilising the existing furniture within your home, such as the top of a wardrobe. If you don't, she will find her own way of getting up high and may get into mischief trying to scale mantelpieces or shelving, knocking down picture frames and trinkets as she goes. If she always wants to jump up onto kitchen worktops, this could explain it. Try placing alternative furniture nearby that you are happy for her to sit on so the worktops are not the only option of getting off the ground in the kitchen. Ideally, you want high places for her in all areas of your home, where practical. It unlocks so much of the space within her territory that all goes to waste if she is stuck on the floor or can only get up on the sofa and nowhere else.

Once she has plenty of space to access within your home, you can begin to think about other resources she needs and uses within her territory – and how to provide these in a way that works best for everyone. Food, water, toys, scratch posts, beds, litter trays, safe hiding places and (if she is allowed outside) access to a cat flap or other access route. There may be additional things that you identify as being important. There is more detail on each of these throughout this book, but here are some general guidelines:

- Keep food, water and litter trays away from busy areas of your home where she may be disturbed.
- Keep food, water and litter trays away from areas where she feels vulnerable, such as near cat flaps, glass doors or near noisy appliances. The number of homes I see with food, water and litter trays placed in a line next to the cat flap would surprise you. Although this could be the most convenient set-up for you, it is unlikely to be the best set-up for your cat.
- Place scratch posts in prominent places and near windows or doors to help her mark her territory.
- Her beds should be provided both up high and on ground level to give her a choice of where to rest. Some cats are very sociable and will love being up on eye level with you. This is another reason why kitchen worktops are so popular, plus they are often rewarded with food and attention when they get there.

- Think about what sort of bed she prefers to sleep in and provide plenty of them. Fig prefers smooth surfaces like a windowsill and will quickly claim a plastic bag if it's left for a moment on the floor. Sparx prefers getting lost under a duvet or snuggling into a really fluffy, squashy cat bed. I need to make sure there are plenty of each throughout my home so they both have a choice of places to sleep that meet their specific needs. This may explain why your cat totally ignores your brand-new, expensive, cushioned cat bed for the box it came in.

11

What Your Cat Wants You to Know about Going Outside

Spending time outside independently is generally something unique to cats – no other pet animal is free to roam away from their home in the same way, without any form of containment. In some ways, this works well for us both; while we are away at work, he can still have his own independent and almost secret life outside the home. He will understand where his home is and, for the most part, return freely of his own accord.

WHAT YOUR CAT DOES OUTSIDE

They engage in various activities in the outside world. Yes, there is a lot of hanging out and bathing in the sunshine – so many cats follow the sunspots both inside and outside the home. However, they also show plenty of natural feline behaviours outside that often can't be performed to the same degree inside. The ability to display natural behaviours is something all animals should have plenty of opportunity to do, for both their physical and mental well-being.

Territorial behaviours

As we've seen, many cats will spray urine to mark the territory outside their home. This is not considered a behaviour problem – which cannot be said if it happened inside. Your cat will be aware that the outside space may be visited by other cats in the area, either passing through or spending time in other gardens, as they may urine-mark here too.

Cats vary in terms of how territorial they are, and this can depend on their temperament, the number of cats there are in the area and can even depend on breed, with the Bengals and Savannas being bred from a very territorial lineage. Some cats will be driven to check in on their outside space throughout the day and may only go out for a few minutes to see what's happening and head back in. Have you ever opened the door for your cat just to find he sniffs the air and changes his mind? Usually, that's all he needs to gain enough information on what's going on outside so he can stay inside, particularly if the weather is poor or there is something outside he is scared of.

Social behaviours

Clients will tell me that their cat is friends with the neighbour's cat and they like to hang out together. In my experience, there is usually more to it than two cats that enjoy each other's company. Some younger cats may enjoy playing together, however, if two unfamiliar cats are spending any length of time together, it is usually because they both want to use a particular part of the garden at the same time and don't mind the other cat being there too.

More often, there is tension between unfamiliar cats in the outside world. Some local cats may try to encroach on your cat's territory and may even try to enter the house. In this case, the behaviour of your cat will determine how this interaction will go. Does he try to drive the invading cat away? Or is he more likely to run back in and hide? Lots of people mention their cat 'lets others in' and stands back while their food is eaten in front of them. It is much more likely the cat is afraid and does not want to risk a fight with the invading cat.

Maintenance behaviours

One of the biggest benefits to your cat going outside is to provide additional opportunities for behaviours that keep him physically and mentally healthy. With the right outside space, there should be multiple areas for him to pee or poo and areas for scratching. This can relieve any tension around litter trays and scratch outlets inside the home and help prevent him toileting or scratching on unwanted objects.

There is more space outside for running, jumping, climbing and hiding, helping to maintain his physical well-being. Hunting is a contentious subject and is discussed in more detail in a later chapter, however, having an opportunity to engage in hunting behaviours is hugely fulfilling for your cat, even if this is limited to chasing bugs or falling leaves. Remember how ingrained this behaviour is into the very nature of the cat. The outside world usually provides more opportunities for this than an indoor environment.

KEEPING YOUR CAT INDOORS

Although I see the benefit of cats having free access outside, I am not against keeping cats indoors. There are, undoubtedly, huge positives to this lifestyle that are difficult to ignore.

- Statistically, indoor cats live longer.
- He will be at less risk of contracting certain diseases such as Feline Leukaemia Virus and Feline Immunodeficiency Virus.
- He will be at less risk of being hurt by another cat. If you have heard cats fighting outside your home, you will know how scary they look and sound. Abscesses and other injuries are common fallouts from cat fights, not to mention the stress these induce, often for both cats. Keeping him indoors will reduce the overall social pressure for all the cats in the area outside.
- He will be at less risk of being stolen, getting stuck somewhere or not being able to find his way home.
- He will be at less risk of being hit by a car. This is the one that my clients quote to me the most.
- A significant benefit is your cat won't kill any wildlife. I am not overlooking this benefit, however, keeping pet cats inside is not an effective method of preserving overall wildlife populations as it is free-living cats that have the most impact here. If this is your sole reason for keeping your cat inside, I would reconsider and give greater thought to your cat's specific needs with regards to an indoor lifestyle.

But there are downsides to keeping your cat permanently inside, which is why this is never an easy debate.

- There is less opportunity for him to display natural behaviour in an exclusively indoor environment, and stress, frustration and boredom can follow. I have seen some fantastic inside environments where cats have so much opportunity for running, climbing, and jumping. Houses with high walkways, perches, rope bridges, cat-sized spiral staircases, even a giant canopy suspended underneath a glass conservatory roof for the cats to sun themselves in total peace and quiet. But these environments are few and far between; not everybody has enough space, finances or inclination to put this in place. There is also extra pressure on you to play with your cat, particularly when he is younger. They need an outlet for that hunting drive, and enthusiastic play sessions are the best way to provide it for a cat kept exclusively indoors.
- The outside world can provide an escape from stressful events in the home. Renovations, busy households or unwanted attention from adults or children can leave your cat feeling like he needs a break. If he doesn't have a safe space to go (which could also be somewhere inside), he won't be able to cope with the stress, affecting his physical and mental health and potentially leading to unwanted behaviours.
- An outside space can expand the territory for a multi-cat household. This can ease competition for space, relieving any tension your cats may be experiencing.

- You will be responsible for providing appropriate litter trays and scratch posts – this is required even with cats with outside access, however, if these are your cat's only options, you must get them right or problems will follow.

- Your cat may experience frustration if he can see another cat from the window but he cannot get outside to chase them away. I have seen plenty of cats that have become so frustrated by this they have begun to urine-mark on the inside of windows and external doors.

- Finally, cats with no experience of the outside world will be less able to cope if they accidentally escape. My mum's Ragdoll, Chitti, escaped one night and we were all out looking for him, calling his name, worried sick. It had only been a few hours, but after it got dark, we found him curled up in a bush only thirty feet or so from our house, too scared to make the short journey home and waiting to be found.

You can see most of the pros are physical, whereas most of the cons are more emotional or concerned with mental well-being, and, essentially, that is what it comes down to. Is it worth risking your cat's physical health to fulfil their emotional needs? And vice versa? Can you meet all their needs inside? For some cats, yes, but for others, no. There is no blanket solution; every cat is different and every environment is different. It is in your hands to find the solution that works for your individual situation.

MAKING YOUR GARDEN CAT FRIENDLY

Some outside spaces provide limited interest for cats, making him less likely to want to spend much time there. He'll either stay inside or head off into someone else's garden. A lot of cats feel intimidated by wide-open spaces, especially if there are other cats in the surrounding area that might want to watch his every move while he's out there. Pristine lawns and concrete courtyards need to be broken up with places to hide, places to explore and ways to get off the ground. You can use garden furniture, shrubbery, potted plants, trees, bushes, sleepers, large rocks, anything that suits your tastes and works well in your garden, checking first that all plants are safe for your cats. Tree stumps are great for scratching, and a sandy area or patch of loose soil will provide a toileting area. It can be useful to include two exits from your home into the garden as cat flaps can become busy areas if you have more than one cat. Your cat should be able to come back into your home at any time, particularly if they commonly fight with other cats, so a microchip cat flap is the securest way for them to come and go freely.

WHEN FREE ACCESS OUTSIDE ISN'T AS EASY AS IT SEEMS

In an ideal world, I would be advocating for all cats to have free and unrestricted access to a safe outside space. However, there are numerous reasons why this just cannot happen or extra consideration is required:

- If your cat has Feline Immunodeficiency Virus. This is a very contagious disease that is transmitted by cats' saliva when they fight. Infected cats should not have unrestricted access outside for the safety of other cats in the area.

- If he has physical or sensory disabilities. This is not a blanket rule, I have met more than a few blind cats who enjoy spending time outside. However, it is something to be conscious of and it may be safer to provide an enclosed space or supervise him while he is out.

- If there are predators in your area. We are lucky in the UK that cats don't encounter predators very often, perhaps foxes are the biggest threat. However, in other areas of the world cats may frequently encounter coyotes, cougars, eagles and other birds of prey, wild dogs and raccoons, and I'm sure there are many others.

- Road traffic accidents are the most common cause of accidental death for cats who go outside. Some will avoid traffic and head in the opposite direction, but others will try to cross, so take this into consideration if you live near a busy road.

- Some cats are not suited to heavy snow or extreme heat. If you have a breed like the Sphynx, with no coat to protect him from the cold, or a long-haired breed such as the Maine Coon or Persian, who may struggle when it is hot, weather conditions will impact on how much time he can spend outdoors.

- If you have restrictions on your property. The decision to give him access outside may be out of your hands due to conditions imposed by landlords, living in a block of flats (first floor or above) or sharing an outside space with other residents.

- Cats are such a popular pet today that shy, nervous felines may struggle to cope with the number of cats in the neighbourhood. If your cat is very nervous of others and is being chased around or intimidated, it can be kinder to restrict his access and keep him inside. Likewise, if he is causing a nuisance to others, going into other cats' houses and eating their food, you need to be accountable for his behaviour. Neuter him, make sure your house is a stress-free zone and always keep a litter tray inside. Microchip cat flaps all round. If that doesn't work, restricting his access outside with a timeshare may be the kindest option for everyone involved, if your cat is OK with that!

There is so much to consider, both in terms of what your individual cat needs and the risks of the outside world. If your cat does go outside by himself, there are a few things to remember to help keep him safe.

- Keep his vaccinations up to date.
- Have regular check-ups with your vet, particularly if he is involved in a lot of fights.
- Keep him inside through the night as he is more likely to be involved in a traffic accident with unexpected vehicles.
- Ensure his microchip details are up to date.
- Neutering is essential to encourage him to stay closer to home and reduce how much he interacts with other cats.
- Arrange a timeshare with another cat owner if you

know there are cats that don't get along.

- Avoid using collars but, if you need to, use a quick-release collar for safety.
- Install a cat flap that reads your cat's microchip and pre-set the times you want him to go out. Be aware of falling into the habit of waiting for him to ask to go out and opening the door for him. This leads to inconsistency – you can't be available all the time – and can cause frustration if you are not able to let him out straight away. I recently worked with a very determined but lovely cat who would bite his owner if she didn't jump up quick enough to open the door.

ALTERNATIVES TO FREE ROAMING

Thankfully, there are now plenty of options for allowing your cat some access outside while keeping him safe. Some are more ethical and cat friendly than others and I will discuss them here.

Secure cat fencing

This usually involves installing additional fencing on top of the existing boundary to your garden to physically prevent your cat from jumping over. This can include wire fencing placed at a 45-degree angle or rolling beams of wood or metal that spin when your cat tries to pull themselves up. I like this option as it allows your cat to use all the natural elements of your garden in its entirety while still allowing you to use the garden as you normally would. If you are experiencing problems with other cats spending time in your garden, secure fencing can help keep them out, but be aware of areas where the neighbour's cat can jump down into the garden but is unable to get out again.

Electric containment systems

Believe it or not, some people use electric fencing to confine their cat to the garden. Here, a wire is installed around the boundaries of the property, often underground to preserve the landscape of the garden. As the cat approaches the invisible wire, a warning sound is heard and, if the cat does not turn back, an electric shock is delivered to the cat's neck through a special collar. This type of containment is highly unethical, as you can imagine. For it to work, it needs to hurt, otherwise the cat won't pay any attention, and, other than the warning sound, there is no clear indication of where the cat can or can't go – it isn't fair on them. To make things worse, other cats can cross the fence freely and your cat will only be able to chase them off up to the boundary. After all this, some determined cats will ignore the shock and still continue to cross the boundary, rendering the fence totally ineffective anyway.

Catios

Catios are large aviary-type enclosures constructed from a wooden or metal frame and secured with a wire mesh or similar. They can be freestanding but are often attached to the outside of the home which works well as you can install a cat flap to give him access when you are not home. You can even use a catio to transform a balcony. They tend to be built on paved areas for practicality, so can offer fewer natural elements compared to accessing the garden as a whole, but they still provide him with significant benefits. They extend the territory so work well in multi-cat households and provide an area of quiet and solitude if they live in a busy or stressful home. Care should be taken to make it a stimulating area and minimise any frustration they may experience at not being able to pass through the mesh. Platforms mounted at various heights, including right at the top, help make the most of the space, as well as places to hide, toys to play with, something to scratch on and even a table and chairs for you to spend time with them, if the space is big enough. Be conscious of other cats approaching the catio as your cat may find this intimidating and will be unable to chase them away.

Harnesses and leads

It is not always practical to install a catio or secure fencing due to finances, landlord restrictions, or there may not be an outside space to accommodate them. Owners in this situation, who still want their cat to experience the outside world, are increasingly taking cats out on a harness and lead. In all honestly, I am not a fan of harnesses and leads. I understand there are certain cats that take well to them and genuinely enjoy accompanying their owners on hikes, into cafes and on holidays. If your cat falls into that category, you are very lucky! However, in my experience, they are in the minority. Many cats don't appreciate being removed from their territory in this way and some are very distressed by wearing the harness, especially if they are not properly trained to wear it (which is a long process of training them to want to wear it, rather than placing it on and waiting for them to get used to it).

Others are very keen to go outside but become frustrated with the restricted movement. A cat's normal behaviour outside does not involve a wander around the pavements. They like hanging out on shed roofs, wandering along fences, hiding in long grass and gravitating towards sunny patches. They establish their own territory boundaries, and they have familiar areas where they will spend most of their time. The opportunity for marking territory outside is limited while they are on a lead, as well as running, jumping, climbing and hunting – all the natural behaviours cats are motivated to perform.

My biggest concern with cats walked on leads and harnesses is they have little or no option for escape. Normally, a cat's primary coping mechanism when they are spooked is to run away, so taking them out into an unpredictable environment, where they are very likely to meet something scary without an opportunity to get away from it, is a welfare concern. For example, dogs have a totally different set of greeting behaviours to cats, and friendly dogs may approach enthusiastically to say hello, while reactive or excitable dogs may try to chase. Furthermore, people will approach to say hello and want to interact with your cat and, again, your cat won't have any opportunity to avoid them or escape.

I do think long leads can be used in a private garden to prevent cats scaling the fences, if necessary. However, they should always be supervised to make sure they don't become tangled in the lead and it needs to be long enough to allow them to enjoy the features of the garden, including appropriate places to hide, and head back inside any time they want to.

Strollers and backpacks

You can buy pushchairs for cats or small dogs with a canvas or netted enclosure in place of a child's seat, or backpacks that you place your cat inside, zip up and carry around on your back. Some of these can be useful to safely transport your cat to the veterinary practice if you do not have a car. However, many of them are not designed with your cat's welfare in mind. For example, some of the backpacks have a clear panel on the front which will leave your cat totally exposed and with nowhere to hide – we know hiding helps cats cope with stress.

Outside of essential travel, backpacks and strollers are being used to take cats on outings to provide additional stimulation and give them some experience of the outside world. As you can imagine, this does not provide any opportunity for your cat to engage in any natural behaviours, but, again, is full of potentially stressful experiences. The unpredictable movement of the bag as the person walks them around may be uncomfortable or even painful, especially as the cat is carried on the person's back and is unable to see objects approaching, including traffic. They are more commonly used in busy urban areas as, by nature, it is more dangerous to give cats free access outside in these spaces compared to rural areas, but it can be noisy and busy and they attract a lot of attention from passers-by. Essentially, the only forms of stimulation they receive from this experience are the sights and sounds they are forced to see, hear and smell, which are likely to be scary or overstimulating. They have no choice in which direction to walk in, which tree to stop and sniff or what to move away from. There is very little comparison to the rich and stimulating experiences had by cats with free access outside. For most, these carriers do more harm than good for the cat's well-being, which is the exact opposite to what they were intended for.

Letting your cat outside can provide real benefits, but care needs to be taken to ensure this is given in a welfare-friendly way, taking account of your cat's needs rather than assuming any time outside is a good thing, regardless of the method. For some cats, and in some environments, living an exclusively indoor lifestyle is a lot less stressful than having enforced access outside, particularly when care is taken to provide an enriched and stimulating inside space.

12

What Your Cat Wants
You to Know about Hunting

Living with an eager hunter and finding the 'presents' they bring home feels like an experience that nobody asked for – or did we?

Cats have gone in and out of favour within human society since their journey into our living rooms began. And the biggest problem they currently face is persecution for their hunting behaviour, mainly due to its impact on wildlife populations. This is ironic, given that humans originally encouraged cats into their households for their ability to hunt rodents.

Your cat is the epitome of the perfect hunter. Whether you have a cute, fluffy Ragdoll or a sleek, athletic Bengal, they will be equipped with razor-sharp claws and pointed teeth primed for catching prey. As a kid, I once saw Spooky catch and eat an entire mouse in my back garden. I was sad and horrified, but also curious to see this ruthless behaviour from the same cat who would sit calmly on my bed at night purring hard and dribbling all over my bedcovers out of contentment.

All cats have an innate tendency to hunt small moving objects, although the motivation to go out and hunt varies between cats. They don't need to be specifically taught how to do this, but they instinctively tend to follow the same sequence of behaviours – locate prey, stalk, pounce, grab and kill/eat. They may adapt this depending on the prey, leaping into the air to catch flying prey rather than forwards to catch a rodent, for example, but generally it is hard wired.

Thanks to effective food storage and modern medicine, your cat's role as pest controller is largely redundant (although it comes in useful on farms and other rural areas). However, it's not fair to expect them to stop hunting altogether because popular opinion among humans has changed and the same behaviours we once encouraged are now considered abhorrent.

WHY HUNTING PERSISTS

You might be wondering why your cat insists on heading out on a hunting expedition when they have more than enough food provided at home? It can appear that she is killing for sport, particularly if she is not even eating her catch just playing with it, and it is this that gets them even more bad press.

We need to remember that cats are not completely domesticated; within a few generations (or less) they can revert from being 100 per cent reliant on people for food, to being completely self-sufficient, and hunting for survival. For this reason, there is no opportunity for their hunting drive to be effectively bred out of them. They are still very much wild animals.

Moreover, not every hunting attempt will be successful, there will be lots of times when their prey gets away. Once they become hungry, their energy stores will be depleting and the chance of a successful hunt will get lower and lower, so they need to take every chance when it arises – even when they are full. This explains the opportunistic tendency we know so well. They are not one of those species that share their prey (the exception being a queen providing food for her kittens), so they can't rely on stronger or more able cats to do the hunting for them. If they want to survive, they need to know how to hunt – so the behaviour is ingrained. Since the urge to hunt is not driven by hunger, it may explain why they might play with their prey rather than eat it.

Outside of this innate tendency, there are a number of factors that might encourage their hunting. They may supplement their diet with prey if there is little variety in their food, not enough food or mealtimes at home are not comfortable for them.

Some cats are simply more outdoorsy than others and therefore encounter prey more frequently than stay-at-home cats. The same can be said for those living in more rural areas where prey is more varied and plentiful. Hunting is opportunistic: almost every cat will be inclined to chase a mouse if it runs past, just as they will chase a bottle top lid across the kitchen floor when one is accidentally dropped.

WHY THEY BRING PREY HOME

If your cat has a tendency to bring prey home and leave it in random places, I feel for you, it's horrible. Thankfully, other than Spooky, my cats have never been avid hunters, although my neighbours' cats have left the occasional pigeon on the driveway! My clients have told me stories of finding mice in their shoes, frogs under the sofas (weeks later), a trail of baby birds down the hallway and – this one makes me cringe – a toddler picking up and playing with a dead mouse they found before their parents did.

Arguably, even worse is bringing home live prey, and if you have had to chase down birds, bats and mice in your home – I honestly don't know what I would do in your shoes.

The reason they bring these home is not because they hate you (which one client told me once) or because they love you (another popular opinion). It's because they see home as a safe place to bring their catch, either with the intention of eating it later (whether they actually do or not) or to play with.

HOW TO REDUCE HUNTING BEHAVIOUR

Restrict outside access

Keeping your cat inside permanently is the only way of reliably preventing her from hunting. However, this is not something I would recommend across the board, as you know. An indoor lifestyle is not one that suits every cat, especially one that has been accustomed to frequent hunting expeditions. The frustration she may experience at suddenly finding herself cooped up inside can cause more problems than it solves as frustration can lead to urine-marking, increased aggression towards people or other pets, and more. If you go down this route, the onus will be on you to make the inside of your home as interesting and stimulating as the outside world, and that's a tall order.

It may be more practical to restrict the time of day she can go outside. Most rodents are active during the night, so you could consider locking the cat flap from sundown to sun up. Again, you will need to safeguard against frustration by giving her food once she is in, providing lots of comfortable sleeping areas and opening the cat flap at a consistent time each morning so she isn't waiting around too long. It will also be important to place a litter tray down overnight (hopefully you will have one already) as it's not fair to make her wait until morning to head out if she needs to pee.

Feeding

Although hunting isn't directly related to hunger, it can be helpful to feed her a diet with a high meat content, little and often. Ensure she has variety in her diet in terms of flavours and textures to keep food novel and more interesting.

Play

Play with toys replicates the same sequences of behaviour as hunting, so increasing the amount you play with her can also help reduce hunting behaviour. If your cat typically doesn't play, we will cover how to encourage this later on.

Bells

Adding bells to your cat's collar can help birds and rodents by alerting them to her presence and giving them an opportunity to escape. This seems like it would work, however, some cats learn to keep very still while watching prey so as not to give the game away. I am also not a fan as another of my childhood cats, Tibby, once got her claw stuck in the tiny gap on the top of the bell and it was really tricky to remove.

Bibs

There is a specific form of collar available that restricts your cat's movements and makes it difficult, if not impossible, to catch birds. I would not recommend these as such a restriction on her movement may make it difficult for her to defend herself if she had a run-in with another cat or prevent her moving through a small space or up onto a high wall.

Remove temptation

Avoid placing any bird feeders or bird baths in the garden. We have all seen our cats chattering at the windows when they see a bird outside, and this is based on frustration. The same goes for window boxes or aviaries nearby. It's just not fair if your cat is driven to catch prey. You can also place strategic cat fencing around tree trunks (usually around six feet high), to prevent your cat climbing up to access birds' nests.

Neuter

Neutering is the biggest way you can help prevent cats impacting wildlife populations. Most prey animals are caught by free-living cats that must hunt in order to survive. Leaving your cat free to reproduce increases the number of kittens born, and those offspring may make their way back into the population of feral or semi-feral cats. Entire cats will also roam further, so their chance of coming across prey animals is higher.

A cat's motivation to hunt is an innate behaviour that has had no chance to be bred out of them and it's unfair to persecute them for performing this natural behaviour. They need understanding and empathy so we can meet their needs in an alternative way, without compromising on their welfare.

13

What Your Cat Wants You to Know about Food

How and what cats eat is a much more complicated subject than it initially seems. In the grand scheme of things, cats have only recently been domesticated to live in human households. Many of their eating behaviour and requirements remain the same as their free-living counterparts, although, as usual, they never fail to surprise me with how they can adapt. There are a few things to keep in mind in terms of feeding your cat.

Your cat is an obligate carnivore. This means he needs meat to survive and cannot thrive on a vegetarian diet. Taurine is an amino acid found in animal protein that is essential for healthy growth and immune function. Although I understand and 100 per cent support humans eating an entirely plant-based diet, it is unethical to impose such a diet on your cat as he can become very unwell and it can eventually be fatal. If you are uncomfortable with providing meat for your pet, I would suggest a cat is not the best match for you.

He needs a diet that is complete and specifically developed for cats. He cannot live on dog food as it does not contain the required amount of taurine, and he cannot live on human food (as much as he may tell you otherwise) as, again, it will not provide him with the necessary nutrients he requires and he needs a much higher meat content than we do.

Cats are unique in that if you don't provide them with the food they need, or in the way they need it, if they have outside access, they have the option of supplementing their diet through hunting or by helping themselves to the cat food left down in the house next door.

WHAT TO FEED YOUR CAT

The best diet will depend on your individual cat's needs and what you can afford. One thing to be sure of: you need to provide a diet marked as 'complete' to ensure all the essential nutrients are included. Generally, the more expensive the food, the better the quality. I recommend going for the best brand you can afford with a protein (such as chicken or fish) as a main ingredient. Try to avoid the very budget brands if you can as these often lack key components of a balanced diet.

Dry food

Kibble comes in a variety of flavours, shapes and sizes. This type of diet has a bad reputation because of the manufacturing process and the additional fillers added to the ingredients, and it has its flaws. However, that is not to say it doesn't have its place in feeding your feline.

Dry food (particularly the higher quality brands) is designed to be complete so he can survive on this food without any detriment to his nutritional needs. For us, it is convenient. It has a long shelf life and it can be left down for him to snack on as and when he wants to (more on this below). It can also be more cost-effective if bought in large quantities. It's easy to place in activity feeders (more about these later too) so can give you an opportunity to make his feeding times more interesting and stimulating.

However, although his basic need may be met with dry food, if this is all he is having, other problems can arise. The water content is minimal in dry food (at around 10 per cent moisture) and, as cats are prone to kidney disease, he will need as much water as he can get to promote healthy kidney function. We also need to think about how dry food meets his behavioural needs and whether this is what he wants to be eating. Most cats I have met show a very obvious preference for wet food over dry, rubbing round their owners' legs while it's being prepared and eating wet food a lot more quickly than dry.

My feeling is: don't rule out dry food, but don't make this all your cat ever gets. Combine it with wet food in a way that works for you both.

Wet food

This is a meat-based food that, again, comes in a variety of flavours and types, including with jelly, gravy or, in some cases, as a pâté, mousse or soup. Most are complete, meeting all your cat's nutritional needs.

Wet food is usually a lot more palatable than dry but, in my experience, there is way too much in a single tin or even a single pouch for them to eat at once (though some cats will scoff the lot). It has a much higher water content (around 75 per cent moisture) so is already better than dry food for this reason. It also works better for older cats who may have dental issues or have teeth removed.

Keep in mind that there are additives included in wet food and the meat content may be lower than you'd expect. Most cats will prefer to eat little and often if they can, and wet food spoils very quickly when left down for them, especially in hot weather. You don't have much option of feeding wet food in any other way than in a regular bowl, so it can mean mealtimes are a bit boring and not very stimulating.

Raw food

Feeding your cat a mix of uncooked ingredients may sound a good idea, given that cats are avid hunters and desire fresh meat. However, as we have seen earlier in this book, the thrill of hunting is in the chase, not just in the eating (sometimes it's ONLY in the chase) so this method of feeding will not be replacing their need to hunt any more than feeding wet or dry food. In practical terms, this way of feeding is difficult to get right and includes a high level of risk for your cat.

If you choose to feed raw, I would recommend buying a commercially prepared diet that you can be sure is totally complete and nutritionally balanced, as it is so difficult to do this if preparing raw food at home yourself. It is also not for the faint-hearted. I recently visited the owner of a Bengal kitten who was given a raw food recipe from the breeder which included beef heart and lung, and chicken kidney and liver, not something they routinely ordered in their weekly online shop or stored in their fridge, and they swapped to a commercial raw diet shortly after she came home.

Commercial raw diets should include instructions on how to prepare and store the food, as there is an increased risk of health problems or diseases if this is not done correctly, some of which can be passed on to humans.

Prescription diets

There are plenty of prescribed diets out there, such as a renal diet to aid kidney function, gastrointestinal diet to help with digestion issues, or thyroid, weight-management, dental and hypoallergenic diets – and I'm sure there are many more. You should always follow the advice of your vet before switching to a prescription diet and change the food over gradually, mixing a little bit more of the new food to the existing diet each day.

Age appropriate

Regardless of whether you choose wet or dry (or a combination of both), it is essential you choose a type appropriate for the age of your cat. Kittens need a different balance of nutrients to adult cats, and senior cats have different needs again. This is another reason I would not recommend raw food – their nutritional needs will change as they develop and mature.

Treats

Treats are excellent for rewarding behaviours you want to encourage (such as walking into a cat carrier) and for strengthening your bond. They can be given to cats in addition to their usual food, but, again, be mindful of what you are giving him. Many commercially available treats are not overly healthy and include additives and fillers, but are OK in moderation. Freeze-dried treats (such as dried chicken or fish) are easily available and are usually 100 per cent protein.

HOW OFTEN TO FEED YOUR CAT

Cats are not designed to eat set meals as humans are. Being natural hunters, they have evolved to eat small meals (small mammals, fish or birds), frequently throughout the day. You can avoid problems around food if you keep this in mind when deciding on how often to feed your cat.

Free feeding

Leaving a bowl of dry food down permanently for your cat to snack on throughout the day is the most convenient approach, but does it work well for the cat? This can only really be done with dry food, so it comes with all the pros and cons of feeding a dry diet. However, if your cat regulates their intake and does not overeat, it gives them total control of their own eating behaviour, which works well for a LOT of cats. They can stick to their natural preference of eating small amounts as and when they want to, and will not experience any frustration from being hungry when food is not available. Free feeding can also reduce tension in a multi-cat household as there is no competition for food or emotions running high around mealtimes.

Of course, this won't work for all cats. Some do not regulate their food intake appropriately and will overeat and become overweight because of it. This is yet another example of where there is no blanket advice that works best for every cat.

Breakfast and dinner

This is my least preferred way of feeding cats but is probably the most common: feeding him when you get up in the morning and again when you come home at the end of the day. This is the least natural way of feeding a cat because they don't eat large amounts of food at once to keep them going all day like we do.

So many people place a whole pouch of food down and watch their cat take a bite and walk away. They begin to worry and assume he doesn't like that food anymore and try more and more types of food until they find themselves gracing him with the most expensive food on the shelf. Have you been there? Me too.

Having said that, breakfast and dinner works for some cats if they have got used to it (adaptable see!), but this way of feeding can lead to changes in your cat's behaviour around mealtimes.

If the first thing you do when you wake up is give him breakfast, you will have a little furry alarm clock for life and his behaviour can become more and more demanding until you give in and get up (more on this below). He may become restless waiting for food to appear and I have seen cats fighting each other in the hour before being fed. I hate to use the term 'hangry', but it fits so well here! Maybe not angry, but frustrated and irritable. It is far too long for him to go without food and you may find he goes off in search of his own food when he can.

Little and often

As you can imagine, feeding your cat small, fresh meals frequently throughout the day (four or five times, if possible) is my recommendation. The main difficulty with this is it's inconvenient, and almost impossible if you are out of the house for long periods – and I totally get this. There are feeders available that open at a set time, but if you are feeding wet food, it is unlikely to stay fresh inside for long.

Sometimes just adding an additional mealtime (splitting their normal amount into smaller portions rather than feeding more overall), can be enough to reduce any frustration around set mealtimes, so feed as often as your schedule permits.

On demand

One thing I would not recommend is only feeding your cat when he asks for it. It is so tempting, and something I have done myself on occasion. They become very good at telling us when they want food, but bear in mind they are opportunistic – they are designed to take food when it is available – so once they know they are in control of when they are fed, this mindset is difficult to shift.

Back to your furry alarm clock. You may be happy to get up and feed him when he wakes you at 6am on a workday, but what about the weekend? Your lie-in will become a battle of wills with your cat, who will do everything in his power to get you up, including scratching on things he shouldn't, knocking things off the bedside tables, pawing at your face (sometimes with claws coming out) and, of course, the constant meow.

He might then decide to try his luck a little bit earlier, so 6am becomes 5.50am, until, eventually, you are woken at 4am every morning. This can be a very difficult problem to resolve, so avoid this situation at all costs. Decide when you are going to feed, and make sure the schedule you choose is going to work for him too.

Whichever diet you decide on, try to mix it up every now and again in terms of flavour and texture to add some more interest to their food. No cat wants the exact same meal day in, day out.

HOW TO FEED YOUR CAT

This may seem like an unnecessary section – surely you just pop the food down in a bowl and leave them to it? There are a few things to keep in mind that can make sure your cat is feeling happy and encourage him to eat more.

No double diners

It is not recommended to keep food next to water because of the risk of contamination – food sometimes makes its way into the water. Double diners are the epitome of this – a single bowl split into two side-by-side sections, one for water and one for food. We have all seen this and no doubt all seen the lone piece of kibble that made its way into the water and has disintegrated into a soggy mess. Avoid these bowls unless you are using both sides for food, and keep water nearby, but not too close to their food.

No plastic bowls

Avoid plastic bowls as toxins contained within the material can leach out into the food. They are difficult to effectively clean, and any scratches in the plastic can harbour bacteria that can be harmful to your cat. Some cats have even been found to show an allergic reaction when using plastic bowls and experience irritation around their chin. It's best to stick to ceramic or stainless steel as, although they are more expensive, they are a lot more hygienic.

Keep food away from vulnerable areas

There are some areas of your cat's territory where they will feel confident and others where they feel more vulnerable. Ideally, we want to make sure their food is kept away from vulnerable points such as near windows or glass doors where they can be overlooked, or near a cat flap where they may be preoccupied with who may be lurking on the other side. Even noisy appliances such as the washing machine can make them feel uncomfortable. Remember, just because your cat eats from these areas doesn't mean this is where he would prefer his food to be and we don't want meal times to become a stressful activity.

It can help to make sure food bowls are positioned away from walls and corners so your cat doesn't have to have his back to the room and he can still keep an eye on what's going on in the territory while eating.

Activity feeding

Cats have evolved to work hard for their food through hunting and will spend much of their time doing so if they are hunting to survive. We are missing an opportunity by providing their food in a standard bowl. Dry food or treats can be placed in activity feeders or puzzle feeders that encourage your cat to use their paws or mouth to release food from the feeder. This can be useful for indoor cats who need additional opportunities to perform natural behaviours inside the home. This is covered in more detail in a later chapter.

Feed cats apart

If you have a multi-cat household, unless your cats are good friends, feed them separately to reduce competition. This can mean providing plenty of bowls of dry food throughout your home (assuming your cats regulate their food intake appropriately), or placing their wet food bowls down in separate areas or rooms until they have all finished.

Microchip feeders

These are covered food bowls that only open for one cat by recognising their unique microchip. They work really well if you have one cat on a prescription diet but your other cat on regular food. It also helps if you have a greedy dog who likes to help herself to your cat's food, but you'll need to make sure she doesn't swoop in once your cat has started eating.

FOOD SCAVENGING

Some cats are determined to help themselves to human food from kitchen worktops, from dinner plates or even out of the bin. This is, again, due to their opportunistic nature – they will take food whenever the situation presents itself, particularly if it is different to their usual meals and if it is very palatable, such as cooked meat or something creamy.

This tendency to take food when it is available is quickly reinforced as soon as the scavenging is successful – the reward of eating the food will encourage him to try again next time, doubling up his efforts when he knows food is potentially available. So be careful feeding him from your plate as you may end up with him pawing at your sandwich as it's going into your mouth.

DRINKING

With kidney and urinary problems so common among the feline population, encouraging water intake is essential to their health. As mentioned previously, dry food has such little moisture content that if your cat is fed exclusively dry, you need to work extra hard at helping him to drink more. As a baseline, he needs to have unrestricted access to fresh water (i.e. replenished daily) at all times.

Avoid milk

Milk is not a suitable drink for cats as most are lactose intolerant and should not be drinking milk at all as your cat may experience stomach pain, vomiting and diarrhoea. Even commercially available cat milk should be given in moderation and not as a replacement for water.

The right container

This can take some trial and error, but different cats like drinking water from different containers. As with food, avoid plastic across the board in favour of glass, steel or ceramic. Some prefer drinking from taller glasses, whereas others prefer wider, shallower bowls. Fill each of these almost to the top so he doesn't have to put his face too far into the glass or bowl to reach the water. This will help you monitor how much water he is drinking too.

The right place

As with food, keep water away from vulnerable places and away from food and litter trays. Provide plenty of different sources of water throughout your home to give lots of choice and make it convenient for him to drink, regardless of where in his territory he likes spending his time. If he is not drinking from a particular bowl, try moving it to another spot.

Drinking preferences

Most cats will drink still water but, in my experience, many will prefer running water over still. In fact, the reason I knew Fig needed to see a vet before he was diagnosed with diabetes was because he was sitting by the kitchen tap constantly waiting for it to be turned on and he would then drink for a long time. He would wait by the tap rather than drink all the water from one of the many bowls throughout the house. So, it's easy to see what he prefers.

There are a variety of cat water fountains available too so you can provide constant running water. I bought a ceramic one for Fig but, of course, typical cat, he still prefers the kitchen tap, but he does drink from one occasionally and so does Sparx.

Other cats may show a preference for rainwater, ponds or puddles, so if you have capacity for this in your home, leaving a container outside to collect rainwater can be helpful here too.

Add water to wet food

If you are worried about your cat's water intake, you can add a small amount of warm water to wet food to help him consume water this way. Most cats won't notice a small amount but be careful not to add too much as you might put him off his food. Some people recommend adding water to dry food to soften it but, in my experience, this has only led them to eat less.

Food and water are survival resources and are of vital importance, but there is no one rule for doing what is best for your cat. Find out what your unique cat likes by offering choices and taking note of what he seems to prefer. This can make a huge difference to his overall physical health and mental well-being.

14

What Your Cat Wants You to Know about Scratching

Probably the most common feline behaviour that causes problems for cat owners is scratching on carpet or furniture. Interestingly though, I am very rarely asked to help with this, which makes me think people see it as an unavoidable part of sharing their lives with a cat. And to some extent, they're not wrong. The scratching itself has several different functions that are instinctual and essential to feline physical and mental well-being – although this doesn't have to be directed at furniture, as we will see.

WHY CATS NEED TO SCRATCH

Claw maintenance

The primary reason cats scratch on posts (or furniture and other surfaces) is to maintain the physical health of their claws. They will embed the claws on their front paws into the post and pull downwards in a rhythmic stropping motion, one paw at a time. Some cats prefer to do this horizontally and you may see the same behaviour performed on a scratch mat or, unfortunately, your carpet instead of a post.

It may appear that the intention is to wear down the claws to keep them from growing too long, and it does help with this, but if you look closely as they pull down on the post you will see the worn, outer layer of the claws is shed, revealing a shiny, sharper claw below: they are sharpening the claws rather than wearing them down. If you find the discarded husks around the base of the post or even stuck to the post itself, this is totally normal. Being predators, evolutionarily speaking, they are motivated to keep their claws sharp, ready for hunting or for defence.

If they don't have access to a designated scratch post, your cat will find somewhere else to scratch; she won't just stop doing it altogether – and neither should she. It is essential she is given an opportunity to perform this natural behaviour; otherwise, the claws can continue to grow, curling round and embedding into the paw pad. This is more common in older cats who are less able to keep on top of maintaining their claws, perhaps due to medical conditions such as arthritis.

Declawing is an abhorrent surgical procedure which is thankfully illegal in many parts of the world, including the UK. It involves removing the bone and claw at the end of each toe. There are numerous physical reasons as to why this operation is bad news for the cat, however, considering their evolutionary motivation to scratch, the frustration they must experience through being unable to perform this behaviour is a huge problem too. We invited a wild animal into our home, and scratching comes with the territory – literally.

Territory marking

There are other reasons why cats are driven to scratch on surfaces. Cats experience these other motivations to different degrees unlike claw maintenance, which is necessary for all cats.

The first of these is territory marking. As you know, cats can define their territory by scratching on prominent objects in the area as the scent glands located in their paws leave their unique blend of scents and pheromones behind.

This is another potential reason why your cat chooses the arm of your sofa for her scratching needs. Sofa arms usually jut out in a very prominent area of the living room – the perfect place to leave a reassuring territory mark.

Stress can increase your cat's urge to mark the territory, so, where possible, take steps to remove or reduce anything in or outside your home that she might find stressful.

Attention seeking

Occasionally, furniture scratching can become a learnt behaviour rather than simply making use of a convenient place to scratch. In this situation, she may deliberately scratch on the most precious item of furniture in your home to get your attention, particularly when scratching a specific piece of furniture makes you immediately jump up, even if it's to shoo her away. Any attention is better than no attention to a sociable cat – they're getting the reward they desire.

I previously worked with a cat who would do this so deliberately it was almost laughable once we recognised what was going on. He had begun to scratch on his own-er's beautiful crushed velvet sofa. He had a suitable scratch post nearby that he was using frequently, and there was no damage to the sofa (yet), so we suspected there was more to this sudden change of target. Cameras revealed he would only scratch the sofa when his owner was home and only when her attention was elsewhere – in the kitchen or watching TV, for example. The moment she heard him scratching the sofa, she would drop everything to stop him, but would then indulge in the most affectionate cuddle session to distract him. It worked in the moment – he did stop – but he had learnt this to be the quickest way to gain her attention. Behaviours that are rewarded will be repeated more frequently!

Frustration

I often joke with my clients that 'no cat likes a closed door'. We have all seen or had cats that, finding themselves closed in or out of a room, begin to scratch at the carpet or on the doors. There is more emotion involved here than regular scratching on a scratch post; they are not happy. In this situation, they are frustrated and may even be anxious. As much as I joke with my clients, there is a truth to this.

Cats are territorial, as we know, so they don't like a closed door. Whatever lies beyond the door is a part of their territory they can no longer access. Sometimes they just want to check in on this part of the home. Often, there are important things on the other side, like a favoured place to sleep – or you. Sometimes they just want to be with you.

One of the most difficult situations is when the cat is closed out of the bedroom at night. I have met lots of people who do this for various reasons, some for health reasons, some for disturbed sleep, some because that's what they've always done. But you can almost certainly guarantee that if your cat can approach your bedroom door and hear you inside, at some stage she will scratch at the door in an attempt to get through. This is a pivotal moment; if you ignore the scratching, she will be less motivated to try it again the next night, eventually giving up altogether when she learns it is futile. However, if you respond, calling out to tell her to stop or, worse, opening the door to prevent her from damaging the carpet, you will have reinforced the scratching and it is much more likely to happen again. In these situations, it is essential you protect your carpet with some sticky-back plastic, a carpet square or a thin sheet of plastic, so you can rest easy at night knowing that if she tries scratching, you can freely ignore it without worrying about your carpets getting ruined. The moment a corner comes loose, she may start to play with it, making things a lot more complicated.

It is so important here to make sure your cat has a comfortable place to sleep away from your door in an area of your home where she feels safe and happy. She may feel vulnerable without you, so put in extra effort to help her settle down for the night. Or, medical reasons aside, let them in. Nothing beats a purry night-time companion, and you may find it's easier to work around any annoying habits she has at night than stopping the scratching. She'll be happier to boot.

PROVIDING THE PERFECT POST

Traditionally, cats are given a post to scratch on with sisal rope coiled around it. Lots of cats take well to this, hence their popularity, however, the truth is that the perfect scratch post may not be a post at all. Here, I will take you through the different options for scratching and how to determine which type will appeal to your cat. You may find an explanation as to why your cat targets the sofas, carpets or even wallpaper, while her perfectly suitable post goes untouched in the corner.

When you are deciding on what scratch post to provide, bear in mind that kittens develop a preference for scratching a certain material before eight weeks of age. It can be useful to ask the breeder or rescue what they have seen the kittens scratching on and you can use this as a starting point. If you have more than one cat, you need to think about what each of your cats needs and wants to scratch on – and this may not be the same thing.

Sisal scratch posts

To maintain their claws, a cat needs to be able to dig in and pull down on the material without it giving way too quickly. Sisal rope works well as it is bound so tightly around a post, although it can be a little too tight at first and you may need to rough up some of the post with a wire brush to encourage her to use it. However, sometimes the fibres of the rope can be a little spiky, which may deter her, so keep an eye on this. Over time, on a well-used post, the rope will become loose and frayed and will need replacing, which is relatively easy to do.

Traditional scratch posts are usually only 40–50 cm tall, which is perfect for a kitten, but a full-grown cat will quickly outgrow this, especially if it's one of the larger breeds. Your cat needs to be able to stretch up to her full height to use the post effectively and be comfortable doing so. The benefit of using sisal rope posts is they allow for the creation of much larger cat trees and towers, with multiple posts on which to scratch at an appropriate height. These towers are a very important part of a cat's indoor territory (see chapter 10), so if your cat uses sisal for scratching, you will be onto a winner with a cat tower.

One downside to sisal posts and towers is they can quickly become wobbly and unsteady. Once a cat has embedded their claws in the sisal rope, particularly if she is stretching up to her full height, she will pull down hard. If the post gives way, even slightly, this will be an unpleasant experience that could deter her from using it in future, and she could revert to maintaining her claws on a large armchair or sofa that is not only the perfect height, but will never give way.

Cardboard scratchers

If your cat has a sisal post and has not shown any interest in using it for scratching, but has a good go on the carpet, you may find she prefers to do her scratching horizontally – many cats do. If this is the case, a cardboard scratcher works very well. This is usually a rectangle of corrugated cardboard bound together on its side, creating a board with plenty of little exposed holes. Cardboard works well as she can dig her claws right in, but small pieces of cardboard will come loose, so it can leave more mess than a traditional post.

This may be a better option for older or arthritic cats that struggle to use a vertical scratch post to properly maintain their claws. They are more affordable than scratch posts, so you can have more than one, and they are easy to move around too, so you can make sure your older cat doesn't have to travel far to reach a scratch-board.

Cardboard scratchers come in many wonderful shapes and sizes, which adds to the appeal for us. My local pet shop stocks various shapes including a large sphere, a pyramid and a cute zebra-print chaise lounge. These are fun but will be a waste of money and space if they are not used, so make sure the one you choose is functional. As with sisal posts, bigger is generally better to add to the sturdiness. If it tips over, it won't be used. If you are limited on space, go for a simple rectangle board, but make sure it is wide enough for your cat to sit on while she scratches so she can weigh it down herself.

I once bought one designed to look like a laptop, with a hinged cardboard lid that lifted up to reveal the corrugated scratch panel underneath. As you can imagine, this was a terrible choice! The lid kept falling on Fig and Sparx when they tried to use it, and, in order to make space for a graphic of a mouse pad, the scratch panel itself was much too small. It did have a small mouse toy on elastic string attached to the side, which I thought was a nice touch and the cats played with for a bit, but all in all it was a complete cardboard scratcher fail and I ended up binning it for something more practical.

Mats

Scratch mats or pads come in a wide variety of shapes and materials, so if this is your cat's preferred surface, it's important to choose the right one. Often, they are already mounted on a sturdy base such as a wooden board, or you can mount them yourself on a sofa arm or table leg or even on the walls. This allows you to place it at your cat's preferred height, and angle it to encourage her to use it instead of an object you do not want her to scratch.

In terms of materials, a few layers of hessian work well; sisal fabric doesn't have the same spiky, tight fibres as sisal rope so can be a better option. Even carpet tiles or cut-offs can be used in strategic areas to provide an acceptable location for scratching and protect the existing carpet if your cat has a tendency to scratch the carpet in front of closed doors. Thick loop pile carpet works better than the cut pile types to allow her to pull back on the carpet more effectively.

Fence posts and tree trunks

If your cat has outside access, she may find outlets for her scratching behaviour in fence posts or tree trunks. Again, this can be performed vertically, though some will scratch on top of fallen logs or along the top of fence panels. This works really well for territory-marking too, and you may see neighbours' cats scratching in your garden, if they have access. Some of these more natural objects can be brought inside your home or specifically purchased for your cat to scratch on. If you have an enclosed outside space such as a 'catio', these logs or small pieces of fencing can be a very useful addition.

WHERE TO PUT THEM

There is more to encouraging good scratching behaviour than simply providing the perfect post, board or mat. Where these are positioned within your cat's territory is as important as the post itself – perhaps even more so.

Convenience

Convenience is often overlooked when it comes to finding a home for a scratch post. The larger ones that are suited to an adult cat are, of course, bulkier and more difficult to place. They can end up in a spare room or in an area of the home where the cat doesn't spend much time. This is problematic as the cat must then make the extra effort to head into another room to scratch, ignoring more convenient objects such as sofas, carpets or armchairs. etc. Most cats will prefer their cat tree to be placed in an area where they spend most of their time, usually in the living areas or a bedroom they choose to sleep in through the day. They should be placed away from anything noisy or potentially scary such as washing machines or tumble dryers.

Your cat will almost always want to have a good stretch and a scratch after waking up from a long nap, so placing a suitable scratching surface near the places she prefers to sleep is a good idea too. This is where cat trees come into their own as, with their multiple platforms, hammocks, hidey holes or cushions, they provide opportunities for sleeping and stretching all in one place.

If you have more than one cat, they may have separate areas in which they prefer to spend time, so make sure they each have a place to scratch that is their material of choice, in a place that is not difficult to reach. If they have to cross paths with a cat they don't get along with, they are more than likely to scratch in a location that is easier and less stressful to reach.

Marking

Because cats mark territory when scratching, leaving their unique scent behind, they tend to target prominent areas. This is true both inside and outside your home. Sofa arms are the perfect example; they are usually located in the living area – a well-used part of the territory – and the sides often poke out into the centre of the room for any cat entering the room to see. That, combined with being heavy and sturdy and covered in a thick, padded material perfect for digging claws into – sofas don't stand a chance!

This is another reason why tucking scratch objects out of the way is counterproductive. Keep in mind that your cat has this motivation to mark territory and think about how you can help her do it in a way that works for you too. For example, some cats like to mark near external exits, so giving her somewhere to scratch in conservatories or near front or back doors will work for her. Others prefer the safest part of the territory, usually your bedroom, and will appreciate a post there so she can keep it heavily marked and smelling familiar and reassuring.

HOW TO ENCOURAGE YOUR CAT TO USE THEIR SCRATCHER

Once you have found the perfect scratcher, and the perfect place to put it, how do you get her to use it? If you have found something she loves, she should naturally gravitate towards it, however, sometimes it is not as easy as that. Under no circumstances is it a good idea to hold your cat's front paws and manually strop them up and down the post. That sounds obvious but I have heard of this happening, particularly when the cat's owner is frustrated with them using the furniture. This method is unlikely to work and risks upsetting your cat.

If she is already scratching on the furniture, temporarily cover the hotspots with a blanket or throw and place your chosen scratcher nearby. Playing with your cat on and around the scratcher is an effective way of encouraging her to investigate and use a post, board or mat. Run a fishing-rod toy up the post or along a board or mat for her to grab and her claws will naturally catch onto the material during the game.

Sprinkling cardboard scratchers or mats with a small amount of dry catnip is very effective too. The catnip falls through the holes and, usually, cats will naturally dig at the holes as part of the catnip response. Before you do this, it is important to know how your cat responds to catnip. If they don't show any reaction, it won't be worth using, and if they become overstimulated or even aggressive as part of their reaction, best to avoid catnip here too.

The truth is I am one of those people who have accepted scratching as an annoying part of sharing my home with cats. Fig and Sparx have claimed more than their fair share of armchair and sofa sides. I know exactly why they do it (the armchair is heavy and the perfect material for getting their claws right into) and I can't blame them. To be honest, I would rather have a few scratches on the arm-chair in our living room than place another cat tree nearby.

15

What Your Cat Wants
You to Know about Litter Trays

It never fails to amaze me that we are essentially living with a wild animal, only partially domesticated, whose behaviour is so enigmatic and wild, and yet for the most part, they are pretty happy to pee in a box. How did we manage to work that one out? However, toileting issues are one of the most common behavioural problems I have been faced with.

Resolving these issues comes down to understanding what your specific cat needs and providing the right toileting area for him. There is no 'one-size-fits-all'. All cats are different and where they want to pee or poo can be a huge source of stress for both you and your cat if you don't get it right.

Peeing outside

If we are all being totally honest, we would love for our cats to do their business outside and away from our home so we don't have to worry about it. Cats that have access to the outside – particularly if they are confident, outdoorsy individuals – usually keep their home clean and free of unpleasant smells. But there are huge downsides to this being their only option and banking on them feeling comfortable with this arrangement. It's my opinion that every cat should have a litter tray inside, to give them the choice of where to go every time.

For a start, if you live in a residential area, chances are you are going to create conflict with your neighbours. Why poo in your own back garden when you can go in someone else's? This was a big problem in my previous home when, on the walk to school last year, I counted over ten ultrasonic cat deterrents on our three-minute walk, two of which had cats loitering nearby. One of these cats constantly pooed in our raised veg box, which was so frustrating even though I could completely understand why – we had essentially created a giant outside litter tray. 'How do I stop other cats pooing in my garden?' is the question I am asked the most, both by those who own cats and those who don't. And it's the question I dread being asked as, unless you are going to completely catproof the fences, there is no sound, ethical way of keeping them out.

Items used as deterrents, such as orange peel, various oils, various spices, metal cat-shaped silhouettes with shiny eyes, ultrasonic deterrents, and the like may work initially, but, in my experience, cats quickly get used to these and learn to ignore them. Throwing water over them or using other methods to scare them away is unfair; they are only doing what comes naturally to them, and it rarely works as they will opt to go when you are not around.

The best way to keep other cats from toileting in someone else's garden is to provide a suitable litter tray inside your home. There may be some cats that still prefer to pee and poo outside, but this will be their choice, rather than you forcing their hand (or paw). You can also make sure your own garden has suitable spots for toileting. A concrete courtyard won't cut it, he will need loose, natural materials such as soil, gravel or sand. If you don't have the right natural space, you can place a litter tray outside (some are designed to be weather proof), or some cats will happily use a large plant pot or bedding tray which can be scooped out to clean, just as you would with a litter tray.

Even with these outside options in place, the biggest issue with expecting him to toilet outside is the risk of stress. Cats need to feel safe while they are toileting. Remember they are a prey species and, while toileting, they are vulnerable. They can't defend themselves easily from predators and it's not ideal to have to run away mid-pee. Everyone's outside space is different and so are the risks. He will need a safe space for toileting and a safe path to get there. If he pees in the field behind your house but can't get to it without passing next door's barking dog, he will be reluctant to go. He may cross paths with other cats, there may be heavy traffic nearby, building work, poor weather (in the cold the ground may be too hard to dig), scary people shooing him away – the list of potential stressors is endless. And everyone's cat is different too, some will take any of these stressors in their stride, confidently pooing in next door's shingle without a second thought; others will be terrified by the prospect of being watched by another cat while peeing. Can your cat confidently handle the challenges of your outside space? If not, you may find he pees inside whether you have a litter tray or not.

If you are still unsure whether to place a litter tray inside your home, use one temporarily and see what happens. If he uses it more often than he goes outside, listen to what he is telling you here – this is his preferred place to go and he will be happier for it. If he uses it occasionally, it indicates there are times when he doesn't feel so confident going outside and having this option to use when he is feeling worried will help keep stress levels to a minimum and avoid those occasional accidents that seem to come out of nowhere. Perhaps it was raining that day, perhaps he had a spat with next door's cat that morning. Let's give him the safe option he needs, even if he only needs it occasionally. Many clients tell me their cat is being lazy in using the litter tray rather than going outside. I prefer to think of it as convenience, and that's OK too! Our home is his home, it's his territory, let's not force him to leave it just because he needs to pee.

Litter trays

Getting the litter trays right is a huge part of resolving situations where cats are peeing on carpets, laminate, sofas, beds, suitcases or anywhere else not designated as a cat toilet. There are many different types of tray out there, some appealing more to owners (with the focus being on disguising the sight and smell of them) and others appealing more to the cat (focusing on how easy they are to use). It can be difficult to get the balance right on what works for us and what works for them, but, ultimately, the priority should be to ensure it works for your cat. Peeing on the floor is much more difficult to live with than a tray that doesn't match the decor. Saying that, there is no tray out there that I can guarantee your cat will use, but there are some general dos and don'ts that can give you the best chance of encouraging good toileting habits from the start.

THE RIGHT TYPE OF TRAY

In my experience, the tray most cats will be happy to use is a basic, large, open-top tray. I say this as it is the easiest for them to use – they can walk in from any direction and have plenty of space to circle around before going and digging in the litter both before and after. The downside to this sort of tray are downsides for us: the smell is not contained, we can see the poo and pee, and the litter is tracked everywhere.

There are plenty of other options that may work better for you or your particular cat, but there may be issues with them that may deter him from using them. Don't forget, he is an individual and what your friend's cat uses or the tray your previous cat used, may not be right for the cat you now share your life with. Here are some options and additional considerations to go with them:

A hooded tray with front opening

These work very well for many cats and some seem to prefer the privacy hooded trays provide. For us, it means the smell and sight of the waste is hidden and it is not so easy for them to kick litter over the sides – although some will give it a good go through the door!

But if it doesn't suit your cat, they're liable to find somewhere else to go. Also, because the waste and smell is hidden, it is easy for us to overlook when it needs cleaning and the smell will be concentrated inside the box. We won't notice the poo left uncovered on top of the litter – but your cat will, and it might lead him to boycott the tray until it's clean.

Most people find they need to remove the cat flap attached to a covered litter tray straight away as this is an additional barrier to going in that isn't really necessary and can put them off using it. Tibby once pushed open the cat-flap with a paw, but changed her mind halfway and closed the cat flap back down onto her paw as she pulled it out, trapping it there. Luckily, I was there to help her release it, but it looked painful!

If a hooded tray is not big enough, he won't be able to easily manoeuvre once inside. I have seen giant Maine Coon cats squash themselves inside tiny boxes, peeing with their face a couple of millimetres from the plastic side of the tray, or comically poking their heads out of the litter tray door. Just because it is physically possible for them to get into, doesn't mean it is comfortable for them to use. Any tray should ideally be at least one and a half times the length of your cat (not including the tail), so if you have a larger breed, be prepared to accommodate very large trays.

If you have more than one cat, you may find one sits on top of the litter tray waiting to ambush the other when he comes out. This experience can be enough to stop him using the tray next time.

A bucket tray with a top opening

This is the ultimate in litter containment. Your cat can kick around in there to his heart's content and the litter will stay inside. However, these are my pet hate because they're such a challenge for cats to use. Imagine them dropping down onto their toilet from above and having to duck down under the lid to dig around and find the right bit of litter to pee on while poking their head through the hole. They are too restrictive for my liking, particularly as a cat gets older and becomes less mobile. If you are already using this tray and your cat is peeing in unwanted places, the first thing I would recommend is swapping this tray out for a large, open one – more than once this has totally resolved the issue for my client.

Trays in cupboards

A relatively new idea is hiding litter trays in cupboards with a side opening to disguise the tray as part of the furniture. I admire the dedication to concealing litter trays and, for the most part, this can be the same as using a regular hooded litter tray, but there are a few extra things to be aware of. If there is lots of space around the litter tray inside the cupboard, chances are the pee is going to miss the tray and end up on the cupboard bottom. Your cat is likely to consider the whole unit his toilet, not just the tray. Be mindful of what else the cupboard is used for. I once had a client place her TV on top of the cupboard, making it noisy and unpleasant for her cat to use.

Self-cleaning litter trays

These are mind-blowing. There are a number of designs now, all of them expensive and most of them unsuitable in terms of space. The smaller ones may fit well in your home but are often too restrictive for your cat to allow space for the self-cleaning mechanism. Some of the larger ones that do provide enough space for your cat are as large as a washing machine. The lengths to which people will go to avoid scooping cat litter never fails to surprise me. Despite my initial concerns, some cats seem to take to these OK, particularly if they tend to avoid trays with any pee or poo in them, but be careful as the sound and movement of the cleaning mechanism can scare your cat (thankfully, most of them have a sensor so it doesn't go off while they are in there).

If your cat is using a simple tray, go with it. There's no need to complicate things and have him jumping through hoops (almost literally!) for our convenience.

THE RIGHT TYPE OF LITTER

Keep it fine and gravelly

Just as there are various types of litter tray, there are also several types of cat litter available to go inside, including those made of clay, paper, silicon or wood pellets. Think carefully about what will work for your specific cat.

Generally, a fine, loose-textured litter that is soft on his paws and easy to rake through is well accepted as this is the type of material his ancestors would have used for toileting. Cats generally dig a hole and cover up their waste, hiding their tracks from any potential predators in the area, so, from an evolutionary perspective, it is their obvious choice. This explains why it is generally very easy to litter-train kittens; they will naturally look for an area that allows them to do this (and their mother will demonstrate this too).

The finer the litter the better, as it will be softer on paws. I tend to avoid wood pellets as they are so clunky and uncomfortable to walk on, especially for younger cats, although they are cheaper than many other types of litter. If you are not sure what litter your cat would choose if they could, you can offer several trays in the same area, each with a different litter, and see which is used the most.

As you might expect, the type of litter you use can influence your cat's toileting behaviour. I have seen cats balance all four paws on the edge of their litter tray with their back end floating over the litter in mid-air, doing everything in their power to avoid having to actually touch the litter.

These little cats are still so determined to use the tray, despite how unpleasant they find it – the total opposite to some others who may flat-out refuse to use it and pee in the bath instead.

Kittens often form a preference for where to pee while they are still with the breeder, which can override the natural preference. As we know, their experiences between two and eight weeks of age will shape their behaviour as adults and, unfortunately, if your kitten has been peeing on the bedding before he comes to you, chances are, this is what he will continue to look for as he gets older.

I recently worked with a lady who bought a kitten from a breeder who used newspaper in the litter trays. He is now five years old and she cannot leave a newspaper on the floor without him heading over and peeing on it. These learning experiences are deeply ingrained and are totally out of our hands. It does mean that you should try to keep to the same type of litter when bringing your kitten home to keep some consistency and establish good toileting habits from the start. You can look to change this later, but it must be done very gradually, as I experienced last year with Sparx. We have three litter trays between our two cats, and use a clay-type litter. I was looking to switch to a more sustainable paper-based litter so swapped one of the trays in one go. I watched him carefully and he went in and out of the new litter, circling round before coming out without peeing. As I watched, he squatted next to the tray and peed on the floor – the first time in thirteen years. It was a face-palm moment for me as, of course, a gradual change in litter is what I always recommend to my clients – adding a handful of the new litter every few days until they get used to it. I was driving around at midnight looking for a 24-hour supermarket that sold our usual type of litter to swap it back before I created a big problem, and he has used the trays consistently since. I haven't made any further attempts to change the litter – my two are fourteen years old and I feel it's unfair of me to ask them to change their habits now.

Keep it clean

You may have chosen the right type of litter for your cat, but if it becomes too dirty, he will find it unpleasant to use and may even forgo the tray altogether. A dirty tray is one of the most common reasons cats pee elsewhere. Different cats have different tolerances for used litter. Some will still use it even if it is very dirty. This is good for us as accidents are less likely to happen, but it isn't nice to make them use a dirty tray. Other cats will have no tolerance for this at all, and will find another place to pee if there is even one pee or poo left in there. As a minimum, solid waste (poos and clumps of pee) should be removed from the tray once a day – or twice, if your cat is fussy. If you use a clumping litter (see below), this will generally be all you need to do as the litter left behind will be clean and you can top up with fresh litter. If you use a non-clumping litter, you will need to frequently empty the whole tray (I would suggest daily) and rinse out the tray itself at least once a week as it will become dirty very quickly.

Before Fig was diagnosed with diabetes, he was drinking a lot more water and peeing much more because of it. My daily scoop of the tray was not keeping it as clean as usual and I noticed a difference in their behaviour in the tray. Instead of going in, circling round, peeing and digging loads after, they were both walking in, peeing and walking straight out. It was clear to me they were uncomfortable with it and it was sad to see them not engage in their normal toileting behaviours. It highlights how important it is to get the litter trays right and make sure your cat is happy to use them, rather than reluctantly using them. I had to up the cleaning until Fig's insulin level was stabilised and he began drinking normally again. So watch your cat's behaviour, what is he trying to tell you? If they dive straight in as soon as the tray is cleaned, they may not be totally happy with how often it is being scooped.

I know keeping litter trays clean can be arduous, especially if you have more than one cat. But it really is worth doing to keep your cat happy and to avoid him looking for another place to pee – getting cat pee out of a duvet or mattress is so much more frustrating. If you really can't keep up, here is where self-cleaning trays come into their own, but make sure it works for your cat, as discussed previously.

Non-clumping vs clumping

It may seem like a non-clumping litter is best for your cat as there won't be lumps of pee for your cat to dig around. However, unless you are changing the entire tray every day, a non-clumping litter will mean leaving stagnant, peed-on litter sitting at the bottom of the tray. The smell can deter them just as much as the clumps (unless you get an expensive type that contains the smell). In my experience, those who use a non-clumping litter don't tend to put much in so there is not so much to throw away. But your cat needs a good 3 to 4 inches of litter to have a good dig around in, and if he can't do that in the tray, he may find somewhere else to rake over his waste such as piles of clothes or bedding.

Removing solid waste from the trays is much easier if you use a clumping litter as you can remove the pee as well as the poo, leaving only fresh litter behind. You need to make sure the litter is deep enough for single clumps to form (3 to 4 inches), otherwise, you will end up with a cemented block of pee-soaked litter at the bottom of the tray.

Litter liners

These are plastic sheets that fit around the base of the litter tray, underneath the litter and over the sides. The idea is to fold up the edges of the liner, lifting out all of the litter for easy disposal. These can seem to make keeping on top of cleaning the trays easier, but, in reality, they don't often work well for your cat. They will keep the bottom of the tray clean, meaning you won't have to wash down the tray itself, and if you are using non-clumping litter, you can easily remove all of the litter in one go without having to precariously tip it all into a bin bag and risk making a mess.

However, if you are using a clumping litter, the liner is essentially pointless – as long as you are keeping on top of removing the clumps and topping up with fresh litter, there is little need to remove all of the litter in one go. The liner itself can put him off using the tray for the following reasons:

- It can be noisy to walk on if there are loose bits.
- Some parts of the liner can cover the litter in the tray making it more difficult for him to dig.
- His claws can get caught in the plastic when trying to dig, ripping the liner and launching pieces of litter in the air around the tray in the process.
- Sometimes they are scented, which he may find unpleasant.

Scented litter and air fresheners

Scented litter products have been created to benefit us, to the detriment of our cats. Cats are so scent-orientated, they define their whole territory through scent-marking and we go and stick lavender-scented litter in the place that is supposed to smell most natural to them. Please don't use it. If you keep up with daily scooping, you won't need to hide any smells with scented litter.

The same thing applies to keeping air fresheners nearby. Your cat is, at best, going to tolerate this. At worst, he will find them unpleasant and you risk him avoiding the area altogether. Definitely avoid placing aerosol types nearby that go off every few minutes. For sensitive cats, the noise can spook them and the scented droplets will be very strong if your cat is there when it goes off. These are added hurdles to encouraging your cat to use the tray, when we want to make it as easy for them as possible.

THE RIGHT PLACE

Location is as important as the type of tray you choose and what litter you place inside it. Much will depend on the layout of your house, the space your cat uses and how busy your household is. Another common cause of cats peeing in unwanted places is because the tray is difficult to get to, for various reasons I will explain below.

Safety

As with outside toileting areas, your cat will want his toilet to feel safe. For this reason, placing the tray in busy areas of the home is not ideal as he may feel vulnerable or spooked by the activity. For example, positioning trays in kitchens or utility rooms works for us as it is easy to sweep up any litter that may find its way onto the floor, and it's a convenient place for us to dispose of the litter. However, these are areas where people are often coming and going, especially if you're anything like me, making copious cups of tea, or my children, going to and from the fridge for snacks. There are constant noises from appliances, such as the hum of the fridge-freezer, as well as noises that are more infrequent like washing machines and tumble driers. In my kitchen, the dog is coming and going too. Your cat may be fine with this, but some are not and it can make every trip to the litter tray feel like a mission they need to psych themselves up for. Is it worth it? Or could they find somewhere easier and safer? Bathrooms can work well, but I wouldn't recommend using the bathroom at the same time as your cat as the flush or shower can put them off – but this does make me laugh as I think about us all queuing outside the bathroom waiting for the cat to finish using the tray!

Another consideration here is your cat may feel more vulnerable around the external exits to your home, especially if he is worried about any neighbourhood cats lurking outside. Keep trays away from external doors, cat flaps and windows, and especially glass doors. If your cat is territorial and fights with other cats or chases them away, he won't want to pee or poo here as he won't be able to defend himself if a rival cat appears at the wrong time. Likewise, if your cat is nervous of other cats, these areas won't feel safe enough for him to pee here comfortably.

Remember there is no right or wrong, I am not saying don't put a tray in the utility room – if it works for your cat, great. But think about where the tray is now, from your cat's point of view. Is there anything around it your cat could find scary? What about the journey to the tray? Is it an easy and stress-free route?

Convenience

This may seem like overkill, but I think it's important for it to be convenient for your cat to use their tray. I have had more than one client living in a three-storey town house with litter trays right up on the top floor, when their cat liked to spend most of their time on the ground floor. One particular client I worked with was not open to placing a tray downstairs, but her cat continued to pee on the dining room floor every day. I convinced her to place a temporary tray down nearby as an experiment and her cat used it consistently. We discussed gradually moving this to a more suitable location now it was being used, but, again, she would not accommodate this as a permanent toilet downstairs. The tray was taken away and, of course, the cat went back to peeing on the carpet. I do understand, no one wants a litter tray on display, but it is part of the package of sharing your life with a cat. It is their home as much as ours and toileting areas need to be part of their territory.

However, care should be taken not to place trays too near to food and water. There's the best Indian restaurant near my house but one table is opposite the toilet doors at the very back and every time my husband and I go with our friends, we always seem to end up at this table. The four of us give each other half-amused, half-exasperated, knowing glances as the waiter leads us over to the same table every time. I don't want to eat my food near the toilets, nor do I want to pee just where I am eating! Or even worse, watch other people going in and out. For cats, there's more to it than just being grossed out: there is the risk of contamination if they pee or poo near to where they eat, so they will either be reluctant to eat here or reluctant to toilet here. Either way, keep them separate to keep them happy.

Add more trays around the house

If you're not sure where to place a tray or you have more than one cat, you may need to add more trays to make it work. Remember the one tray for each cat, plus one extra rule? It is common for cats to prefer one area for peeing and one for pooing, so two trays may be better than one for your single cat. The benefit of providing additional trays is it allows you to experiment with the location and helps you to see which ones he tends to use more, getting an idea of where he would prefer his trays to be positioned. If you have one in the kitchen already and then provide one upstairs in the bathroom, does he continue to use the one in the kitchen? Or does he swap to using the one upstairs? If so, you can see he would prefer to keep that one permanently. If he uses both, you may want to keep the additional tray as well as it will mean each tray has less pee in it before it is cleaned.

When we lived in a town house, Fig and Sparx had two trays separated on the top floor and one on the bottom floor in a small toilet that was used infrequently. They used to pee in the top ones and poo in the bottom one (the one we affectionately called the 'poo tray'). This worked perfectly for them. It gave them the option of heading to a different tray if one was difficult to get to for some reason or already being used by the other cat. The areas we picked were quiet, away from food and water and generally near areas where they liked to spend time – they used all parts of the home at different times of the day.

There are so many factors to get right when it comes to litter trays and there is no one-size-fits-all – cats are all different and have different needs in this respect. Look at your home from your cat's point of view – how can you make it easy for him? Prevention is better than cure when it comes to toileting issues so get it right from the start before peeing on the carpet becomes a habit that you cannot break.

16

What Your Cat Wants You to Know about Multi-Cat Households

Tension between cats in multi-cat households is something I see very often, and it is one of the problems cat owners struggle with the most. Many people will tolerate aggression towards themselves and toileting in unwanted places (although you are not doing your cat any favours by ignoring it), but to see your cat getting hurt or terrorised by another cat in your home is very upsetting and difficult to ignore, particularly if you decided to bring a new cat home and now they are not getting along – the guilt is real.

Not every cat is capable of living with other cats. Some will flat-out refuse to share their territory and will attack others on sight. Others will show their reluctance to share by urine-marking inside the home to help the territory feel more like their own again. Some may avoid other cats at all costs, meaning their activities are limited as they spend so much time hiding. If your cat shows this extreme response to any cat they meet, it is probably a sign that she would prefer to live as a single cat.

In most cases, it is not so clear cut and the dynamics between both cats will determine whether they get along, as well as the environment and a careful introduction. In this section we will look at the natural social behaviour of domestic cats to understand what our cats need to live in harmonious multi-cat households.

NATURAL SOCIAL BEHAVIOUR OF FREE-LIVING CATS

What's fascinating about feral feline colonies is that they choose to cohabit in a group rather than live a solitary life. We know they don't need to live with other cats to survive, they continue to go off and hunt alone and do not bring their catches back to share with the rest of the colony, except to provide for kittens. So, what is it that makes them stay? It could be that colonies are usually congregated around a plentiful food source where there is ample opportunity for hunting. There also needs to be enough safe shelter to accommodate all the cats in the colony. The moment there is competition for food and shelter, individuals may begin to leave. Another reason is that there could be greater protection from predators in that there are more cats to defend the colony. But more interestingly, colonies often consist of related females who frequently share nursing duties and kittens will feed from numerous lactating queens. That is not to say that females are more likely to get along than males in your home, as most pet cats are neutered and neutering removes any potential sex differences when it comes to the social behaviour of that individual.

It is not the case that colony cats just happen to be in the same place at the same time. They engage in friendly behaviours that help with social cohesion and bonding. These behaviours are exactly what you want to see with your cats at home and include:

Allo-grooming

This is where two or more cats will lick each other's fur in the same way as they groom themselves. This should be mutual, as one cat licking another may not be well received by the cat that suddenly finds itself being licked.

Allo-rubbing

When cats rub against each other to share a mutual scent. The tails may wrap around each other if they do this while walking.

Allo-resting

Cats rest near each other, usually with one resting their head on the other or curling up together.

Play

This is especially common in younger cats, and playing together is a sign of a positive relationship. The play should be relatively equal in terms of who is chasing and who is running, claws should be sheathed and there should be no vocalisations or signs of distress, unless it gets out of hand.

Signs they are not getting along too well include:

Avoidance

They may try to keep out of each other's way and may even leave the colony.

Aggressive vocalisations

They may hiss at another cat in an attempt to get them to move away. They may also growl or yowl, or caterwaul if a fight ensues.

Fighting

There may be intense staring between the cats, and one may try and move off in slow motion to get out of this situation without inciting a chase. Physical fights between outside cats are often over very quickly, but can be very serious.

Signs of stress

Generally, these cats may show signs they are unhappy being part of the colony. This could include walking with their belly on the ground, tail swishing, ears going back, their fur might stand up and they may swallow or lick their lips frequently.

HOW DOES THIS COMPARE TO OUR PET CATS THAT LIVE TOGETHER?

The biggest difference between free-roaming cats and those that live with us is that free-living cats have a huge amount of control over their lives. They have choices. They can decide who they live with or who to avoid, when to spend time near the colony or when to go further afield. With our cats, we make those choices for them. We decide which cats live together and try to make it work even if they are incompatible and don't get along, and often there is little opportunity to keep them apart. Feeling in control is such an important part of being a cat.

Cats with access outside will sometimes decide to leave home of their own accord if they are not happy and take up residence in another home nearby. Of course, the thought of this is upsetting for us, but it is natural for them to want to take themselves out of a situation they are not happy in and we need to listen to what they are trying to tell us. I have had plenty of clients whose cat just moved themselves in and it can indicate they were living in a stressful environment before and are looking for something more relaxing. Keeping cats indoors means there is no option of escape and as much as we want to keep our cats home and together, it can be stressful for all cats involved to be confined to a home with cats they don't get along with. Stress-related illnesses can follow and can have a big impact on the physical and emotional health of your cats.

However, the choices are not just to let your cat leave home or shut them in together. There are ways to help them accept each other and there are plenty of multi-cat households where all cats are happy and content living alongside each other. So how do we get there?

Consider why you want another cat

Bringing a new cat into your family is a big step and there are plenty of reasons why you might want to add a new feline friend. That said, there are several reasons where I would advise caution.

To improve your existing cat's behaviour

This is something that I am asked about time and time again. If your cat is showing a behaviour problem such as aggression, toileting issues or anything else, adding a new cat to the mix is very unlikely to resolve the problem. There may be times when it helps. For example, the behaviour of lone kittens can be challenging, so a similarly matched playmate can help. But most behaviour problems have a stress element, and, for the majority of cats, adding another to the home is likely to exacerbate stress, even if it goes well, so the likelihood is it will make the behaviour worse.

To replace one part of a bonded pair

It is heart warming to see two cats so closely bonded. I have been so lucky that Fig and Sparx have bonded so well, and I often come home to find them squidged up together in a squashy armchair. It is also heartbreaking to see that bond come to an end and cats will grieve the loss of a companion, and the changes in the environment and routines that come with it. It is totally understandable to want to fill this gap, but it very rarely goes well – feline relationships are so delicate. Grief is not the same as loneliness. They will be grieving the loss of that particular individual and to replace them with a strange cat is like expecting a human to replace a lost best friend with a total stranger. Give your cat a chance to adjust to the change and settle down again, which can take many months. Then think about whether the time is right for adding a new addition, or whether bringing a new cat home is a good idea at all. The guilt of getting this wrong and introducing a new cat as a companion for your first, only to find you've made them even more miserable is a heavy burden.

To replace one part of a non-bonded pair

This is also not a great idea but for a different reason. Many cats will tolerate living with another cat but would prefer to live life as a single cat. When one cat is lost, watch the behaviour of your remaining cat. If there was tension between them, often you will see her confidence grow and her behaviour blossom. Suddenly, she starts sleeping in places she never slept before, becoming more sociable and generally seems happier than ever. Again, that is not to say you should never get another cat, but listen to what your cat is telling you, and do not be too quick off the mark to replace a lost cat because you are worried your remaining cat is lonely. You should want to bring a new cat home because you want a new cat in your life and it's the right time for you and your family, including your existing cat.

Are you ready for another cat?

With so many cats looking for homes, it would be wonderful if you could help them all with no negative consequences. However, there are factors to consider making sure you can accommodate a second (or third, or fourth!) cat.

Space

Cats are territorial. Each individual needs to feel they have their own space, unless they're so bonded with another cat that they function as a single social group and are happy to share the same space and resources. When you bring a new cat home, they may form a social group, but this will take time. Consider whether you have enough space to allow both cats to have separate territories within your home. This might be a permanent set-up if your cats don't get along and prefer to keep out of each other's way.

Additional resources

On a similar note, if your cats do not get along too well, they won't always be comfortable sharing important resources such as food bowls, water bowls, litter trays, beds, cat trees and more. You may need to provide additional resources throughout your home to accommodate this and make sure there is enough to go round. The general guidance is one of each per cat, plus one more, to ensure all cats have a choice of which litter tray to use (for example). It will help reduce competition and help them live separately in the same home, so be prepared to double up on all those bits and bobs – and it will cost you in terms of both money and space. If you have a five-cat household, it will need to look like you have a five-cat household, and this much cat furniture is not for everyone.

Time

To give your cats the best chance of getting along well, a slow and gradual introduction is usually necessary. Yes, there are people who have thrown their cats together and they will tell you it worked out, but there are plenty more where this has gone pear-shaped and the cats have got off on the wrong foot. Even when the cats do manage to work it out themselves, the experience is stressful for all concerned. Be prepared to spend several weeks slowly integrating your new cat into the household.

The relationship between cats you already have

I have visited plenty of houses with multiple cats who already have tense relationships and are uncomfortable living together but are getting by. This is not an ideal situation, and the cats are often experiencing some degree of stress here. Adding another cat to this sort of environment is not something I would recommend. The social pressure will already be too much for some of the cats in the household and it will only get worse with another cat in the mix. Behaviour problems are rife in this sort of environment.

SETTING UP FOR SUCCESS

There are several things to consider before choosing your next cat and finding the right match for your home.

Previous experiences with other cats

It is sometimes difficult to know how your cat will react to another cat joining the family. Her behaviour around other cats can help you understand how she will feel once you introduce a newcomer. The relationship will depend on numerous factors, and your cat may get along with some cats and not with others. However, her general behaviour towards other cats can give you an idea as to how accommodating she will be towards a new cat joining the household. For example, does she tense up and become agitated every time she sees a cat through the window? Does she actively fight with other cats outside? Has she shared her home with a cat in the past that she did not get along with? If yes, it is reasonable to assume she won't be thrilled with the idea of a strange cat permanently living in her home and the introduction process may take longer than it would for a cat that is more relaxed and easy-going around unfamiliar cats. Similarly, we want to find out how your potential new cat feels about other cats too, so ask the breeder or rescue about their experiences so far and their behaviour around other adult cats. If they show any negative behaviours such as hissing, tensing up or recoiling from the scent, this can indicate they will be wary of sharing a territory and you may need to move much more slowly with your integrations – this may not be a good match at all.

Male or female

Clients will often ask me if they should adopt a male or female next, or they have existing views that two males will not work as well as two females. This seems to make sense as wild colonies usually consist of related females. However, if both cats are neutered (unless neutered very late in life), gender is largely irrelevant, and you are wasting your energies committing to either a male or female rather than focusing on finding a cat whose temperament will be compatible with your existing cat.

Neutered or entire

On the subject of neutering, your chances of successfully integrating a new cat to your home will be much higher if both cats are neutered (and kittens neutered as early as possible). This is because the behaviour of an entire (a cat that is not neutered) male or female will be different to their neutered counterparts. With sex hormones in play, your entire cat will be primarily concerned with finding a mate and may view other cats as competition, increasing the risk of tension or aggression.

Kitten or adult

Generally speaking, kittens are usually accepted more readily than adult cats. If kittens are well socialised, happy and confident, they are unlikely to show hostile behaviour towards your existing cat, so you are already halfway there. Additionally, because they are not so territorial when very young, they are not so much of a threat and your cat has less reason to feel hostile towards them. That being said, kittens are cute and lovable, but, wow, are they annoying at times! And, undoubtedly, your sensible grown-up cat will feel the same way towards them as you do in those early months. You will need to put in the time to play with your kitten a LOT to protect your adult cat from taking the brunt of all your kitten's energy. Other cats are a lot more fun to play with than stationary toys as they are moving targets and when they are chased, sometimes they will run – so much fun for your kitten.

Health

The wellness of both cats involved will influence how well they get along too. If your current cat is suffering from a health condition that affects her well-being, such as osteo-arthritis or another painful condition, it is probably not the right time to introduce a new cat to the home. The experience of suddenly sharing a territory with a new cat is a stressful one and it may potentially affect her health. There are circumstances when this can still work, but additional time and energy needs to be given to finding the right match (this is an example of where bouncy, enthusiastic, playful kittens are not such a good match) and helping to give your cat more space to take herself off when she needs to.

Temperament

Once you have found a cat or litter of kittens that meets all the criteria to work for your current cat, you now need to find the perfect temperament. This is a difficult one to advise on, as there are no hard-and-fast rules of what will work and what won't. Think about what your cat would want in a new companion. Is she young and playful and looking for a playmate? If so, you could look for a kitten who enjoys playing with his or her littermates and perhaps not the shy kitten who is hanging back from the rest. Or is your current cat calm and timid? In this case, a similarly calm kitten or cat would fit in much better than a more boisterous individual that seems full of beans.

Realistic expectations

If you bring home a new cat, you undoubtedly want him to make friends with your existing cat and for them to share a happy life together. Unfortunately, in my experience, it is actually quite rare for two unfamiliar adult cats to closely bond and engage in all those lovely, friendly behaviours such as mutual grooming and sleeping curled up together. Even two cats sleeping apart from each other on the same sofa or same bed are usually not bonded. These are generally the best spots in the house and often they just both want to sleep there, it doesn't mean they want to do that together. If you are lucky enough to have a genuinely bonded pair, you are in the minority and, realistically, most cats in multi-cat households tend to consider themselves housemates rather than family – two cats living separate lives in the same house. And that's still a successful outcome, as long as they are happy individuals and able to keep out of each other's way when they want to.

A CAREFUL INTRODUCTION

Remember cats are both predators and prey, and this shapes their whole perception of the world. They have evolved with an inherent need to protect themselves from harm, so they are fit enough to hunt, but also need total control and awareness within their territory to flee from potential predators. Adding a new cat to the home upsets the equilibrium, changes the dynamic within the home and means your cat needs to adjust her behaviour to accommodate the new addition. Very rarely do cats take well to a new housemate right away, particularly if they are both adult cats.

A slow introduction allows you to gradually get your cat used to the idea of sharing their home with another cat. It involves a series of small steps that are easy for both cats to adjust to rather than expecting them to immediately be OK sharing their whole home with a stranger.

A few noes . . .

Avoid 'letting them get on with it'

Yes, there are people that threw their cats together and will say it worked out fine. But what is their definition of fine? If you ask more questions about the behaviour of both cats, you'll usually hear there was some initial hissing, maybe growling. They may have had a chase or a fight. But (if they were lucky) eventually, they decided to keep out of each other's way and things settled down. This doesn't sound like it went well to me. Maybe for two kittens, it might go more smoothly, (although I still wouldn't recommend it), but for most adult cats this experience will be super-stressful, and we know stress can trigger behaviour problems and have a detrimental impact on your cat's physical and mental well-being. Why risk it? A slow introduction is more time-consuming/inconvenient for us, but it is a kinder process for your cat.

Avoid using crates and carriers

Another potential method of introducing cats is to shut one in a dog crate or cat carrier and let the other cat(s) investigate without the risk of any physical aggression. Please, please do not use this method for introductions, even with kittens. I have seen this go wrong time after time and it can be extremely distressing for the confined cat. One case that comes to mind involved a lady introducing an eighth cat to her home. On the day she brought her new cat home, she placed the carrier on the floor and encouraged all seven cats to come and say hi. I understand why – she was focusing on preventing physical fights, but did not consider how each cat would be feeling in this situation. Needless to say, the cat inside the carrier was so distressed; she was hissing, spitting and yowling, desperate to escape but unable to go anywhere. The other cats were already wary of a new cat and did not respond well to her distressing behaviour, and it was upsetting for all cats involved. This is the opposite of how you want your cats to be feeling when they meet. Let's set them up for success, not failure.

Feeding meals together and moving their bowls closer

This is generally not bad advice and meals can be very useful as tools in a successful introduction. However, it must be done carefully, as part of a bigger introduction plan. Too often people will feed their unfamiliar cats in the same room and move them closer each day until they are eating side by side. This is much too close for them to

183

be while eating, even when they actually like each other. Remember they are solitary hunters and so solitary eaters. There is no need for them to get this close and you risk replacing the positive association between food and the other cat, with the discomfort of them eating too close.

I once worked with a man who was worried his cats weren't getting along so well. They were hissing at each other and having the odd fight here and there. He began feeding them treats and luring them closer together using the food. His aim was for them to associate the other cat with the tasty food. Unfortunately, as he was giving the treats, the cats were hissing and swiping at each other more than ever, and the fighting happened much more frequently. The experience of 'treat time' was causing a further breakdown in their relationship because the only reason they were coming together was because they wanted the treats, not because they liked each other, and this turned into a negative experience for them every day. We will talk about the most effective way to use food as part of the introduction process later on.

Now on to the yeses . . .

Let me take you through how I aim to introduce cats. I say 'aim' because it almost never goes to plan – the road to a successful integration is full of ups and downs. This is why it helps to work with a feline behaviourist throughout the introduction process. We can troubleshoot along the way, take steps forwards or backwards where we need to and can work through any curve balls your cat throws in (which they will).

Let your cat settle in before beginning

Be it a kitten or an adult cat joining your home, he will feel unsettled and potentially anxious when he arrives. He may have just left his litter, or a safe and familiar rescue pen. He won't be in any frame of mind to meet another cat at this point and needs time to relax and settle in.

Designate part of your home exclusively for your new cat. This could be a bedroom or another room in your home but take care to ensure your cats can't see each other. Try to make this a room your existing cat won't miss so she isn't put out about it suddenly being closed off, although I know this is easier said than done sometimes.

Helping your new cat settle is a priority at this stage, so make sure he has everything he needs such as lots of places to sleep – blankets and smaller beds are ideal and you will also need these later – places to hide, his own litter tray, scratch post, food and water. Spend plenty of time in there with him and watch his behaviour. He may hide at first and take his time to come out, but once he is moving through the room confidently and showing relaxed and friendly behaviours towards you, you are ready to move on.

Work with their scent

Remember how important scent is for cats. They use it to define their territory by facial-marking and leaving their scent behind where they sleep and scratch. It is also used to communicate with other cats without them having to meet, so we can use this as the first step to 'introduce' the cats in a safe and risk-free way.

You can do this by swapping some of their beds around – here is where those blankets and beds come in handy. Don't swap them all at once, just one or two at a time. Leave them in the room for the other cat to investigate – we want them both to feel in control throughout this process so if they want to sniff it they can, if not, that's fine too.

Watch their behaviour when they do investigate the blankets. Some cats will hiss or recoil a little after sniffing. This isn't ideal and indicates things may take a bit longer than you expect. If they ignore the blanket, that's a great sign – we will take indifference over hostility! If they sleep in the bed or rub against it, that's even better.

You can also stroke your cat wearing a glove or using a cotton cloth, and then leave this in the other cat's room for investigation and vice versa. Do not stroke them with the same glove or cloth, as this will be too overwhelming for them.

We are looking for both cats to get used to the scent of the other without hissing or recoiling from the scent on the bed or cloth.

Let your new cat explore the rest of your home safely

Your new cat will be acclimatising to your home as well as getting familiar with the people and animals within it. He will need time to explore the other parts of his new home without encountering your other cat. It can take some logistical planning but with your first cat confined to another part of the home, you can let your new cat out of his room and explore when he is ready. You could do this one room at a time for now. This will help your new cat feel more comfortable and will help future meetings go more smoothly. We don't want your new cat to be worrying about meeting your first cat while still getting used to a new area of your home. We are breaking it down into as smaller parts as possible.

This will also help mix their scent too, as your new cat sleeps in the same beds and scratches on the same cat trees as your other cat, just at different times. We are slowly beginning to get both cats used to the idea of sharing a territory in a very low-pressure and easy-to-accept way.

Meeting through a barrier

Once your cats are familiar with each other's scent and are comfortable time-sharing the home, we can start to introduce short, controlled meetings through a barrier. The barrier is to allow your cats to interact safely while we gauge how their interactions go and can get an idea of how they feel towards each other. This stops any potential chases or fights, but it also helps your cats feel more confident during the meetings. Remember cats prefer to avoid conflict so without the barrier, they may try and run at this point. The reassurance of the barrier will help them stay and get to know each other.

Barriers can be difficult to make work in your home. Baby gates are often recommended but I find these tricky as some cats can slip through or others can jump over, so may need some adjusting. A door cracked open a few inches (with a stopper to prevent them being pushed open) can work OK but encourages cats to approach and stick their noses or paws through. If you are lucky enough to have a glass internal door, these work well, or doorway dust barriers are available from most hardware companies. These are temporary plastic doorway covers that usually have a zip opening to allow you to get through.

Cover the top of the barrier at first by draping a blanket over a gate or pinning up a sheet of fabric, leaving a small gap at the bottom to control how much of the other cat they can see and make sure they are not overwhelmed. This can be gradually lifted an inch or so at a time over several sessions, until your cats can see each other fully. Install the barrier in a doorway where both cats feel comfortable and relaxed on their respective sides.

At first, we want both cats distracted but reassured. It is not ideal for them both to run up to the barrier as this can scare the other cat off. Use treats and toys and have a person on either side of the barrier so they can make it a positive experience. If this isn't possible, use your cats' mealtimes to keep them distracted, but keep them a good distance from the door, a couple of metres or whatever works in your home. Avoid placing the food near the barrier as this forces them together when they are not ready. We want them to choose to do this in their own time and on their own terms.

Again, watch their behaviour. What is happening? Are there any aggressive vocalisations – hissing, growling, yowling? What is their body language like? Are they relaxed with an upright tail? Confidently playing with you or accepting treats? Or are they fixated on the other cat? Eyes staring and body tense? If you are seeing negative signs, encourage them even further from the barrier (or the other cat further from the barrier on their side) until you reach a point where both cats are comfortable.

If they are looking more relaxed, you can gradually allow them to approach the barrier over several sessions, again, keeping a close eye on their body language and behaviour.

Meeting this way may take place over a few days or weeks. You should aim for at least once a day for a few minutes at a time, longer if they are both relaxed, but you must continue to supervise. Every cat is different, there are no hard-and-fast rules as to how long this will take, but as long as you are making progress and the cats are showing signs of relaxing around each other, keep going.

Supervised meetings without a barrier

Don't be tempted to move too quickly to this step. It is easy to have a really positive barrier meeting and try opening the barrier, only to find things take a backwards step. Prepare in advance so you can set them up for success.

Go back to very short meetings, just a minute or so, as this is a new challenge that your cats may feel uncomfortable with. The longer you leave them together, the more chance there is for things to go wrong, so, at this early stage, short and sweet is best to help build up a foundation of positive meetings that their relationship can grow from.

Choose a time of day when they are both calm and sleepy and open the door between them while they are both distracted (and not ready and waiting to burst through). Make sure there are plenty of high places, hiding places and comfortable beds for them in this area. Once they are in the same room, feed them a meal (or use treats if they like these more) at separate ends to keep them distracted, and stop the meeting shortly afterwards. This may seem pointless as they haven't really interacted at this stage, but we are gradually hinting at the idea of them being in the same room together here, just being in the same room is enough. Do not just sit back and see what happens. Almost certainly one will approach the other and you will lose control of the meeting very quickly.

If you need to separate them and your distractions aren't working, place a large pillow between them to block eye contact and prevent a chase. Do not sit between them unless you are confident there is not going to be any aggression and do not pick them up during a chase or fight as any aggression may potentially be redirected to yourself.

Once you have a few of these meetings under your belt, you can begin to give them more freedom around each other. When they have finished eating, give them a chance to wander off a little, but be proactive – if one heads straight towards the other, step in with a distraction of treats or toys. Reward them sporadically with treats when they are being calm and relaxed. Here, you will get a gauge for how each of them is feeling. If they permanently try to get to one another, it's going to take more time until they can be left unsupervised. If they do their own thing and head off to sit on the sofa or climb a cat tree, this is an excellent sign. Encourage them to avoid and ignore each other. If one or both cats settle down into a bed or on your lap, you are good to keep this meeting going until one of them wakes up again and this is where you can really begin to make progress with them living together.

Giving them free access

Once they start having supervised periods of time together, things usually move very quickly from this stage as they no longer want to be separated and they want to have free access around their territory. Continue to supervise them for as long as you need but you will quickly get an idea of how they are feeling towards each other and if there is any risk of aggression between them. I would recommend continuing to separate them at night and when you are not home if you are worried, but this will soon become unnecessary the longer you go without any aggression.

PROBLEMS YOU MIGHT ENCOUNTER DURING INTRODUCTIONS

Escapees

This seems to happen at least once with every cat family I am helping. Why do cats turn into slippery little fish when you are trying to move through a doorway without them getting past? If this happens, don't panic; locate your cat, and separate them again, using a pillow to keep them apart if there has been a chase or fight.

As much as my heart sinks when I hear this has happened, it often gives us a lot of information we can learn from. Sometimes, the cat escapes, sees the other cat, totally ignores him and carries on with his day. In this case, it is a really good sign that things are going well, and we can afford to perhaps move a little more quickly through the process. If there has been a full-on fight, it means we must go back a step (or steps) and suggests things need to move even more slowly, or (depending on how severe the attack is) perhaps these two cats are not right for each other.

I once worked with a lady and her cat who spent his entire time on edge and ready to attack the new cat that had recently joined his home. As soon as the door to his room was opened for someone to slip in, he was determined to get out. He managed it on the day I visited (after I had left – ready to set up an introduction plan for them). He found the new cat in an instant and attacked so severely he drew blood with both his teeth and claws. After this incident, we had a long discussion and decided it was not fair to put either cat through the introduction plan. Her first cat was finding it too stressful and the risk of injury was so high that it was best for her new cat to find another home.

Meetings that go wrong

Sometimes your perfectly planned meeting goes badly, and you end up going back a step. This is usually because your distractions and rewards are not exciting enough for your cat. You can be shaking your bag of Dreamies but he may totally ignore them and still make a beeline for your other cat. Really take the time to find what works for your cats. This could be tuna, cooked chicken, ham, liquid treats, springy toys, moving toys, feathers, the list is endless.

Again, learn from the experience and work around it. I recently worked with a couple introducing a kitten to their adult cat. We were at the stage where they were meeting for the first time without a barrier. We discussed it and decided to keep the door open so the older cat could choose to leave if she wanted to. What unfolded was the kitten made a dash for the door, which made the older cat chase him – all down the stairs and behind a chair in another room. They were able to separate them easily and there was no aggression, but we learnt from this that the door needed to be closed, and extra hiding places and escape areas added inside the room.

Stressful events

Life still happens around the weeks of introducing your cats. If either cat falls unwell, or there are changes to the environment that cause stress or anxiety, it can affect the success of the integration. For example, next door's cat might enter your home unannounced or you might have a gathering of people over. Try to minimise changes where you can, but if it's unavoidable, put meetings on hold until everything has settled down again.

Cats that struggle being separated

Keeping them separated during the introduction period is a necessary evil. You have to do it to prevent things going wrong, but, as we know, cats are territorial and do not appreciate being denied access to some of their territory. No cat likes a closed door, remember.

Once your new cat has spent enough time around you and in the rest of the house, they will begin to feel frustrated being shut in a single room and no doubt you will be exhausted from trying to share your time between your cats. At this stage, the sooner we can move to supervised time together with no barrier the better, while still moving carefully.

On a similar note, what tends to happen here is both cats will be calm and sleepy when they are separated, but as soon as you start a meeting, they wake up and are active and full of energy. This is a wasted opportunity; we want them to spend their downtime together rather than apart as it is so good for their relationship to see the other one calm and relaxed. This is why it is so important to have plenty of beds and resting areas and encourage them to settle during the meetings, when you can.

SET THEM UP FOR LONG-TERM SUCCESS

This section aims to help your cats get along after the introduction process and can help if you are having issues between your cats that already live together.

Reduce feelings of competition

Free-living cats will only stay together if they think there is ample food and shelter. I say 'if they think' because it doesn't matter if you know you would never let your cat go hungry or without a comfy bed, what matters is their perception, and whether food and shelter is something they need to worry about. Let's take food. If you feed your cats side by side and one often eats from the other's bowl, chances are one cat will feel their food is at risk and competition begins to rise. Just because there is no fighting at mealtimes, we can't assume everyone is happy with this arrangement. Some people will tell me their cat steps back and lets the other one eat from the bowl – this is problematic as the cat stepping back is usually doing so to avoid conflict, not because they don't want to eat. Feeding them separately or free feeding with multiple bowls if they regulate their food intake appropriately will help all cats feel better about the availability of food.

Competition for resting areas is often overlooked but is super-important for cats. The 'one per cat, plus one' rule of thumb does not apply here – your cats will sleep in more than one bed, so you want loads and loads of them. And think about what each of your cats like – warm and cosy, smooth and cool, high up, inside a box – they all have their preferences. If you notice there is tension around a particular area, such as the top of a cat tree, radiator bed or hidey hole, throw in a couple more to offer alternatives and reduce the competition around this area.

For all other resources such as litter trays, scratch posts or water bowls, the more the better, but stick to one for each cat, plus one, placed in separate areas.

Be proactive

If you notice tension rising between your cats, step in to help get them back on track. The more negative interactions they have, the higher the risk of their relationship deteriorating and things begin to snowball, with every interaction ending up (or starting) with a hiss or swipe. Help restore the balance by increasing the number of positive interactions using food to reward calm behaviour and toys to defuse the tension. Get things spiralling in a positive direction instead.

Encourage avoidance

This one seems nonsensical, I know. But cats need to feel like they are in control and things are on their terms. If you encourage them to spend their time apart by providing cat-friendly spaces throughout the entirety of your home, interactions between your cats will be on their terms and at a time when they are ready to meet rather than because they are both forced to sleep on the bed because there are no other places to sleep that are this comfortable. This takes the pressure off and helps them feel more tolerant of each other.

Provide a complete set of feline resources in separate areas to allow them to establish individual territories if they need to, and ensure they aren't forced to cross paths to access what they need. The cat flap is a good example of how the set-up of the home can influence their relationships. In many homes, one cat may prefer to spend their time upstairs, while the other spends more time downstairs. However, there is usually only a single cat flap, located on the ground floor of the home, meaning the cat upstairs will be forced to walk through the territory of the other cat to gain access outside. If there is tension between the cats, this means the upstairs cat could be ambushed on her way in or out of the home. Look at your home from each cat's perspective and try to identify where the challenges lie and how you can overcome these by setting up your home differently. They may prefer a cat flap at the other side of the house, or even a route down from the upstairs window.

DON'T SEE REHOMING AS A FAILURE

I am not suggesting one cat needs to rehomed if there is any sign of tension. Ideally, we want all cats to be happy, but, in many cases, housemates rather than family works well and the odd moment of tension here and there is manageable. However, we need to be open to rehoming if it is in the interest of one or both cats.

Some cats feel trapped and miserable in a multi-cat household. Some can't fully rest or relax unless they are tucked as far under the bed as they can get. Some are so worried about drawing attention to themselves, they pee under the bed or in a quiet corner instead of making their way to a tray. They are permanently on edge and can't engage in normal feline behaviours for fear of being attacked, stalked or watched.

And for cats that are permanently on the attack (and not being playful) – it's never because they're nasty cats; they're anxious too. They can't rest or relax easily – they always feel their territory needs defending. They are hypervigilant and can't engage in normal feline behaviours as they don't feel comfortable sharing their territory. They might be urine-marking and attacking on sight – this is not what any cat wants day in, day out.

Rehoming is not something I take lightly or recommend without exhausting all options and considering the risks to all involved. I know rescues are full, often with long waiting lists, but we need to be objective where we can and look at life from the cats' point of view.

If it comes to rehoming, as difficult as this will be, please remember you haven't failed them. You are putting their needs first and making the heartbreaking decision to find them a better living situation that works for them. That is a hard thing to do, but a sign of a truly amazing cat care-giver. Find a reputable rescue centre and be honest with them about your cat's behaviour, they will help them find a happy home.

17

What Your Cat Wants You to Know about Human Interactions

There are plenty of ways to interact with your cat and build your relationship. Some cats will be more open to human interaction than others, and this is influenced by your cat's personality, their physical well-being, your behaviour and the environment they find themselves in.

A slow blink – the 'in'

Most cats naturally find eye contact or staring intimidating, be it with another cat, or a person. Blinking your eyes slowly is a very clear method of letting your cat know that your intentions are good and you are not a threat. Often, they will do it back to you and some will blink slowly at other cats too if they are friendly. A slow blink is the perfect way for anyone to greet a cat.

I use this method of communication every time I meet a new cat I am working with. It's an ideal way to let them know from a distance that I am friendly. I find it so reassuring when they blink back at me; I know that I am 'in' with them and, if they are an aggressive cat, I can breathe a sigh of relief knowing I am probably not in any immediate danger.

Stroking

When most people see a cat, the first thing they want to do is stroke them. I know I do. When you come across a friendly cat that loves being stroked by everybody, it is a joyful experience. But in actuality, cats that love any form of human interaction are few and far between. Most have their likes, dislikes and tolerance thresholds, just as we do too, and it can take time to learn about what your cat wants from you. To build a strong relationship with him, where he trusts you and feels comfortable being stroked, all physical interactions need to be on his terms, at least at first.

- Start with the slow blink, with every cat, every time. It really helps and if you get one back, it's a great start.
- Call him over to you. As cats like to feel in control, we want him to approach us rather than the other way round. This way, we know he is in a sociable mood.
- Hold out your hand in front of him and wait for him to approach. Avoid reaching down towards him to stroke the top of his head, he may find it scary and many cats may turn their head and bite you.
- When he approaches, give him time to sniff you and wait for him to stop. This is SO important. Once he

has sniffed, watch his behaviour. If he turns away, he is not looking to be stroked right now, so don't try to stroke him. If he rubs his face on your hand, you are good to go! We have a running joke in my family that every cat hates my brother as he's always getting himself swiped or hissed at. He just needs to give them more time to sniff him. He goes in for a stroke too quickly and ends up with an itchy scratch.

- Focus stroking around his head. As they have scent glands on several areas of their face (including cheeks, chin and the area above their eyes), they are particularly receptive to being stroked on these areas. Stroke in the direction of the fur and avoid touching his tummy or base of his tail until you know your cat very well and can be certain he enjoys it.

- Check in with him frequently. Cats prefer short interactions rather than long-drawn-out stroking sessions. Stop every few seconds and watch how he behaves. Does he take the opportunity to move away? In which case, he's probably had enough. Does he turn back to you and encourage you to carry on with a head bunt or face rub? If so, you are good to carry on, repeatedly checking in every so often.

- Watch his body language. Some like being around people, even on laps, but don't like being stroked. Others tolerate it for a while, but can lash out quickly once it gets too much. Watch for signs he is losing patience such as a twitching or swishing tail, ears turning back, pupils dilating, fur rippling, sharply turning his head towards your hand, attempting to bite (he may just touch the skin with teeth) or swiping.

I always laugh that cats are a lesson in consent, but it is absolutely true. If you do your own thing without listening to what they want by watching their behaviour, you will lose their trust.

Headbutting

Some sociable cats will approach and attempt to rub their head on your hand or face. This is a friendly behaviour and a sign that your cat really enjoys your company. Fig would do this for hours if he could and it is a wonderful way of interacting with him. Everything is on their terms, and they have total control here, embrace it!

Picking up

Cats are just the right size for us to pick up and cuddle, but do they genuinely enjoy it? For some friendly and sociable cats, yes, they may. And if you lift and hold them in a manner they are comfortable with, that's not a problem. However, so many people misunderstand how their cat feels about being picked up, or, worse, they don't care. Cats being held this way are responsible for so many internet videos of cats swiping at the face of the person holding them and branded an angry cat.

Being lifted and held does not fit with the natural behaviour of a cat. As a prey species, they like to feel in control of their movements. All feelings of safety will be lost once all four of their paws leave the floor and they will feel vulnerable. If you are not sure if a cat likes being picked up, it is best not to try until you know them well.

If you do decide to pick them up, place one hand behind their front legs to support their chest, and the other hand under the back paws as you lift to support them there too. Do not be tempted to scoop them up and flip them over onto their back as here is where you are likely to be met with a wriggling bundle of legs and claws, struggling to get down. Respond to their body language and if they attempt to jump down, let them go.

Talking

Talking to your cat is a very low-pressure way of interacting and is great for those who are more on the nervous side and need time to build trust. Although he can't understand what we are saying, he can recognise his name and will respond more to your voice than that of a stranger. Lots of cats will respond to their owner's voice with a cute meow and most of us cat people love having little conversations with our cats.

Playing

Most cats love to play, particularly when they are younger. It can work well to build your cat's confidence around you if they aren't overly tactile. If you are trying to make friends with a cat who is still quite nervous around people, play can be the perfect way to build your relationship.

Grooming

Some cats absolutely LOVE being brushed. Use the same careful technique referred to above in the section on stroking to make sure they are happy throughout.

Training

Cats can be trained to do any number of behaviours, which can be functional (such as training to enter a carrier) or more for fun (such as training to sit or lie down) and can be an enjoyable and stimulating activity. Training should only be done using techniques based on positive reinforcement to help them stay happy and motivated throughout the training sessions.

Be mindful of the behaviours you train. I taught Fig and Sparx to stand up on their back paws for treats a good twelve years ago now for a university project. To this day, they will still try their luck and stand on their back feet in the hope I will reward them with a little piece of ham, bless them. This behaviour isn't a problem for me, but be careful of teaching 'paw' or 'high five' as it encourage them to ask for food by pawing, and, if you don't give it to them, frustration will set in and they will gently try with their claws out to see if that works. It may be gentle and in no way aggressive, but it still hurts if they touch your skin!

18

What Your Cat Wants
You to Know about Children

Cats can be amazing companions for children. I had some very special cats as a child, and my children have bonded closely with Fig and Sparx. My four-year-old loves it when Sparx squishes up next to her on the bed and it's sweet to see her tiny hands gently stroking his head. However, kids (particularly younger children) can be unpredictable in their behaviour and although this is totally understandable, it can make them difficult for your cat to be around. Kids don't instinctively follow the rules of cat-friendly handling because they look so cute and cuddly. This can mean your cat becomes uncomfortable around children and may respond aggressively when a child approaches to touch them. Even my super-friendly Fig is known as the 'angry cat' among my children's friends as he once hissed at my daughter's friend who got too close too quickly.

Many cats will remove themselves from the situation if they feel uncomfortable around children, but if they feel trapped and unable to escape, they may bite or scratch. If your cat is known to show aggression, you may want to seek help from an experienced cat behaviourist to help understand why and what to do about it. Cat bites and scratches can cause deep wounds which would be upsetting for any child to experience. The biggest danger comes from the high risk of infection. Cat teeth are small and sharp and carry a large amount of bacteria. Bites often cause small puncture wounds that seal over quickly, trapping the bacteria inside. Infection can follow within a few hours, which, if left untreated, can have serious consequences.

If you have children in your home (or expect to within your cat's lifetime), it is essential you take the time to help your cat feel comfortable around children and help children behave sensibly around your cat. This can be done in three ways.

1. Socialisation. When choosing your cat, find a kitten or a rescue that has had good experiences with children in the past, either during their socialisation window with their mother, or has a track record of living happily with children previously. Remember, the socialisation window has already closed when you bring your kitten home, so you cannot wait until then to socialise your kitten with children. This is covered in more detail in a previous section.

2. Preparation. Cats don't like change. So, if you are expecting a baby or children will be coming into your life shortly for any reason, help your cat adjust to the changes these children will bring. This is covered below.

3. Education. It will be your responsibility to teach any children how to behave around your cat. Some cats are more comfortable than others, and you will need to know their thresholds.

PREPARING FOR A NEW BABY

If you are expecting a baby, this will bring a considerable amount of change for your cat. However, newborns are easy to be around (compared to toddlers) and it is very uncommon for cats to injure an immobile infant – in fact, I have never met a cat that has done it. It is the changes to the territory that tend to upset cats at this stage, rather than the actual presence of the baby. Big changes can mean your cat feels stressed and this can lead to problems such as urine-marking – something no one wants to be dealing with, especially with a baby in tow. As with any changes, helping them adjust to smaller, easy-to-manage changes will help them cope a lot better than everything happening at once. Here are some of the things to gradually expose to your cat when you are expecting a baby.

New smells

Remember your cat's territory is defined by scent, so encountering unfamiliar smells at home can be stressful. You may wish to start using small amounts of the creams, bubble baths, wipes, etc., you expect to use with the baby. Let them investigate in their own time and learn they are nothing to worry about.

New sounds

Babies come with musical play gyms and toys that squeak, jingle or rattle. Gently expose your cat to these noises by playing them in a separate room so she can hear them at a low volume, a safe distance away. She may or may not come and investigate which is fine. Once she is comfortable with this, you can allow her to investigate these toys when she wants to, but always take care not to startle her.

You can do the same with low levels of babies crying, by finding online soundbites to help them become accustomed to the crying too. Gradually increase the volume, but not too loud. You may find your cat takes herself off when your baby cries, and that's not a bad thing.

New objects

This is a time when you will be bringing home new furniture and making other large changes to the environment. Bear in mind that these will also come with new smells that can unsettle your cat so keep her away from these at first until the smell fades. Aim to stagger installing new furniture (cots, Moses basket, bouncy chair, etc.), so she can familiarise herself with these without becoming overwhelmed. Allow her to investigate furniture in her own time. It is a good sign if she facial-marks the furniture as it will help her recognise this new item as a safe part of her territory.

Redecorating

If you are planning to redecorate the nursery or any other part of your home before the baby arrives, the sooner you can do this the better. Redecorating often changes the entire scent profile of the room which can really unsettle your cat. Keep her away from this area for a few days until any strong fumes have had a chance to disperse and place some familiar items back in the room before she explores again, such as her bed or blankets she has slept on, a cat tree or armchair. These items will smell normal and will provide some reassurance, helping her cope with the change.

Routines

Changes in routine can be stressful for your cat, especially if her current routine has been fairly consistent. If you are planning to change who feeds her, scoops the litter tray or mainly interacts with her, try to make these changes now so she can adjust before the baby comes. Some changes can be for the better and I found my cats loved having me home while I was on maternity leave with my first daughter.

LIFE WITH A NEW BABY

Once your baby arrives, the biggest change for your cat is likely to be the change in your behaviour as you focus more on the baby. It may be difficult to give your cat the same amount of attention she is used to, and she may now be closed out of rooms she was previously able to access, such as your bedroom overnight or your baby's nursery. The frustration she will experience with you on the inside while she is on the outside may cause her to either vocalise loudly outside your bedroom door, scratch at the carpet or at the door itself, or both. Tackle this early as it is the last thing you want to hear when you've just got your baby off to sleep!

I found Fig and Sparx a massive comfort throughout my journey into motherhood and, even now, I will find pockets of quiet time with them when I need five minutes' calm – they really are amazing companions.

19

What Your Cat Wants
You to Know about Dogs

You would be right in thinking I am a cat person, but, of course, I love dogs too and introduced Bucky, a fox-red Labrador puppy, to Fig and Sparx in 2020. Bucky is the first dog I've had and to say it was a shock to the system is an understatement, as I'm sure a lot of first-time puppy owners would say too. Introducing Bucky to the cats and establishing a harmonious household long-term was one of my priorities (alongside giving Bucky a happy home and teaching my children to be sensible around him). Let's face it, no cat is desperately hoping you will bring home a puppy, so it's best to do it only if it's the right time for your family, you feel your cat can cope with the significant changes a dog or puppy will bring to his territory and you have the time to appropriately manage your new dog around your cat.

DIFFERENCES BETWEEN CATS AND DOGS

Understanding the unique natures of cats and dogs can help you identify the challenges you may experience when they share a home and can help you encourage a positive relationship between them right from the start.

Dogs are inherently social as a species and long to be part of a group, so have developed complex ways of communicating with other dogs. They will often greet each other immediately while sniffing the other dog's rear end. No cat is ever going to take kindly to that! Dogs also display appeasement behaviours to tell the other dog they are not threatening and minimise the risk of conflict, such as licking, turning away and holding their tail low. Your cat will not understand the intention behind the behaviours your dogs displays, nor does he (for the most part) display any appeasement behaviours himself. Being descended from a solitary species means they have had no use for appeasement behaviours and will tend to run away to avoid conflict. So, their communication is lost in translation with dogs geared towards forming social connections. Cats often take a lot longer to trust other animals or people, especially if they are already adults when they meet their first dog. This can mean your cat permanently camps out upstairs once your dog moves in, even if the dog is only trying to be friendly.

WHAT DOG SHOULD YOU CHOOSE?

There are several factors to consider when choosing the right dog for your home and lifestyle, and finding the one that is going to have the best chance of getting along with your cat.

Age

You may wonder whether it is better to bring home a puppy or a rescue dog. I would say that the nature of the animals you are working with matters more than their ages. Unless an adult dog is very reactive around cats, you will generally find the process more challenging with a puppy, as their own development means their behaviour is changing all the time and you may need to adapt your behaviour to maintain the relationship between your dog and your cat. Don't let age be your deciding factor, find a dog or puppy with a temperament that works for you and your family, your cat included.

Experience

It is not enough for a dog to have lived with a cat before. You need to know the nature of the relationship and the behaviour of both animals when they were together. If you are bringing home a puppy, the behaviour of the pup's mother will be important too. If her puppies are watching her chase cats from the garden, they will be learning that this is the right thing to do and will be more likely to do it themselves.

In your dog's previous home, how much did she see of the cat? Were they snuggling up in front of the fire together? Or was the cat desperately trying to sneak past her without being seen? Was she barking at the cat? Trying to play with him? Chasing him? These situations are so common: the cat just tries to stay out of the dogs' way to cope, but this dog will be labelled as 'able to live with cats'. Be careful and ask questions.

Breed

There are no defined rules on which breeds of dog will be OK with cats and vice versa as so much depends on their individual temperaments and unique experiences both as puppies and kittens, and as mature animals. There is often a lot of variation between dogs of the same breed in terms of their personality and behaviour. However, there are certain breed traits to be aware of that may make integrating the two much more challenging and you may be set up to fail at the first hurdle if you opt for a more challenging breed.

For example, historically, dogs in the hound breed group (such as the Greyhound), herding dogs (such as the Border Collie) and terriers (such as the Border Terrier – one of my favourite breeds) have all been bred to either chase, seek out or kill small animals. Not to say this would happen to your cat, and I know there are plenty of households out there that have made this work. However, it does mean there may be much more management involved, more active training of your dog's behaviour around your cat and, in some cases, a permanent separation allowing them to live separate lives in the same house. I feel this raises questions of whether it is ethical for a prey-driven dog to live with a cat, in terms of the welfare of both the cat and the dog.

Invest time in choosing the right dog for your home and look for a temperament that feels like it would fit well with everybody. If you have a frantic puppy that does everything at 100 miles per hour and is on the go all the time (regardless of breed), your cat is going to struggle to spend much time with her before being spooked. Of course, all puppies have moments like this, but, generally, if you can find a dog or puppy with a calmer, more placid temperament, this will make things a lot easier for your cat.

INTEGRATING YOUR DOG
WITH YOUR CAT

Cats thrive on consistency. For the most part, they can struggle with changes to the home, routine and social interactions and you can guarantee bringing a new dog into the household is going to upset all three. With a puppy, the introduction process will generally take longer than with an adult dog (depending on the temperaments of your cat and your dog) because, as mentioned above, puppies are constantly changing. Just when you think you've got there, your pup brings a new challenge for you and your cat to work around. It was two years before I felt comfortable to leave Bucky alone with Fig and Sparx, once he had finally become an (almost) sensible grown-up Lab. Here is some advice on successfully integrating your dog into your home without upsetting your cat.

Preparation is key

Create small changes

Just like with a new baby, adjusting to a new canine companion means getting your cat used to all the things your dog needs to help her settle in and feel at home right away. This may include multiple dog beds, new food and water stations, a crate or a pen, plenty of dog toys, leads, harnesses, poo bags, puppy pads, the list goes on. Bringing all this home at the same time as your dog can be too much for your cat. Each of these objects can be brought into your home well before your dog arrives, giving your cat time to adjust to these items being there without too much concern. Small easy changes are much easier to process than multiple changes at once.

Introduce scent first

As cats are so scent-orientated, try introducing your cat to the smell of your new dog well before she moves in. You can do this by taking a small blanket or cotton cloth with you every time you visit your dog or puppy in either the rescue centre or breeder's home. Hold the blanket as you interact with your dog (if she is comfortable with it), so the blanket retains her scent. Once home, leave it on your sofa or another part of your living area for your cat to investigate in his own time. There is no need to place it near him or rub it on him; just as when introducing cats, he will be a lot more comfortable if you allow him to investigate it in his own time.

Set up your home strategically –
Give them both a safe space

Your cat will need to have access to parts of your home that your dog cannot get to, at least at first, to stop them meeting accidentally. Your dog will also need her own space to go where she won't be randomly disturbed by your cat so she can settle in. Decide which area of your home you are going to give your dog access to before she arrives so you can prepare in advance. You can use stair gates to restrict your dog's access, as your cat should be able to slip through. If you are using a pen or crate for your dog, ensure this isn't too disruptive for your cat. For example, avoid placing it in an area that he needs to walk past to get to his food or litter tray. Think about how he uses the space in your home and keep this in mind when setting up the territory to accommodate your dog. If you need to move the food bowls or litter trays to make it work logistically, do this as early as possible before your dog arrives to get them used to it in good time. The set-up needs to work for both your cat and your dog – I may be team cat, but I want your dog to be happy too.

Keep them apart

Initially, you will need to keep your dog separate from your cat(s) to avoid accidental/spontaneous meetings you are not prepared for. When a new cat joins your household, it is easy to confine them to a spare room for a few days to give them time to settle in before starting to introduce them to your other cats and the remaining parts of the home. However, this isn't practical with dogs. They are social animals and need to be with you for most of their day. This means you may have to confine your cat instead to avoid them crossing paths, so you need to give the logistics of this lots of thought. When Bucky joined our home, we were living in a townhouse which worked perfectly as our living room was on the first floor, with our kitchen downstairs alongside another comfortable seating area. This allowed us to give Bucky the bottom floor and garden, and the cats the top two floors, which suited them just fine.

We would usually spend our evenings in the living room upstairs, but to help Bucky settle in we stayed downstairs for the first few evenings (and nights). Fig was often on the other side of the kitchen door meowing to come in, so there was some frustration on his part. We tried to split our time between the cats and Bucky as much as we could manage to keep them all happy.

Getting them together

Your tools to set up for success

It happens too often that people decide to allow their cat and dog to meet, open the doors and sit back to see how it goes. More often than not, this will end badly as, when left to their own devices, your dog is likely to get excited and your cat is likely to get scared. It is commonly advised to let them scratch your dog and 'show them who's boss' from the start. Although I understand why this is popular advice, it is not something I would recommend. If it works, it means your cat was upset enough to be aggressive to your dog – so he's unhappy – and it must hurt your dog (or scare her enough) for her to learn to avoid your cat in future – so she's not happy either. We want to encourage them to develop a good relationship from the start, so they can feel comfortable around each other and be relaxed sharing the same home.

You need to be proactive when introducing your dog and cat. It is up to you to make sure the meetings go well, and, for the most part, this involves controlling the dog's behaviour around your cat and ensuring she doesn't get too close. Remember, a cat's default behaviour when they are scared is to run away – so he shouldn't be bothering your dog unless your dog is bothering him, either by coming over to say hi or wanting to chase him. You have to take the heat off your cat and teach your dog how to behave around him.

Here are the things that will help:

- **A reliable recall.** You MUST be able to call your dog away from your cat the moment you can see she is getting too close and making your cat uncomfortable. Pre-empt it, if possible.
- **Long-lasting chews.** The best thing about Bucky is that, being a Lab, food is his favourite thing and a stuffed Kong or yak's, milk bar would make him forget all about the cats (for all of ten minutes). Find or make something that really appeals to your dog.
- **Walks.** If you know your dog will sleep for a good hour after her walk, use this time for them to meet as

your dog's behaviour will be more manageable.

- **Leads, crates and pens**. Your dog needs to be restrained at first to stop her running over to say hello to your cat. If she is comfortable in a crate and pen, you can use these, but do not use them if not. And do not allow your cat to approach the crate and scare your dog, it's not fair on her. Encourage them to spend time apart in the same room as they will both feel a lot more comfortable.
- **Play and training with you**. Make yourself more fun and interesting than your cat during the meetings. Play with your dog or teach her a new trick to keep her happy and entertained while your cat is in the same room.
- **Baby gates or pet gates**. Mentioned previously, these will help you manage their movements and prevent any impromptu meetings happening while they are still getting used to each other.
- **High places for your cat**. Give your cat a place to be where he can see your dog from a safe place.
- **Comfortable resting areas for them both.** If you can encourage one or both animals to settle down for a rest or sleep, the meeting will be a lot smoother and probably a lot longer than if they are awake and active.

The first meeting

The common saying – 'first impressions count' – is as relevant to cats as it is to people. The first meeting is extremely influential in determining how your cat feels about your dog and vice versa. You need it to go well.

When you first bring your dog home, go in without her first and check where your cat is. Close him in a bedroom or another part of your home where he is relaxed and comfortable and then bring your dog inside. I have known plenty of clients come home with their puppy in their arms, to a friendly greeting from their unsuspecting cat who suddenly notices the puppy, panics, and disappears under the bed. This is a not a good start, and it will be much harder to help your cat accept your dog after such a jolting first meeting.

Before introducing them, give your dog time to settle in. We gave it a couple of days. Bucky was playing, sleeping, cuddling, eating, drinking and toileting all normally almost immediately. This may take longer if you have taken in a rescue dog, particularly if they are quite nervous or just taking their time to find their confidence in a new home.

Plan for the first meeting so you can set them up for success. Your dog needs to be restrained in some way to keep control of the meeting – a lead, a pen, a crate – but it is important she feels comfortable with this, so find what works best for her. Your cat is unlikely to be comfortable with too much (or any) attention from your dog, so, even if you are sure she will be friendly towards your cat, at this stage, we want to avoid them getting too close. Even approaching for a sniff would be too much.

Being less of a social species than dogs, your cat needs to be in control of the meeting so he feels confident. Choose a time when your dog is calm and sleepy and (with her placed on a lead, or in a pen) open the door and allow your cat to come in, in his own time. Have distractions to hand to prevent your cat approaching your dog and unsettling her too. Keep meetings short in the early days and try to end on a positive note, even if you are tempted to carry on.

Once Bucky was sound asleep in his large pen after a busy day of playing, we opened the door and Fig, being more confident and sociable than Sparx, headed straight in. Fig wandered in, gave Bucky's pen a wide berth and headed over to me and my husband on the sofa to park himself on the back of it. It was a super-calm meeting; Bucky was easy for Fig to be around (being asleep!) and Fig could come and go as he pleased. We gave him some treats and some attention (which he loves), to reassure him and make it a nice experience for him. When Bucky woke up, we distracted him with treats to keep him happy too and stop him paying Fig too much attention. Sparx did not appear at all, and that was OK. If I had gone to get him and carried him into the room, he would have panicked and ran back upstairs; it had to be zero pressure and his decision to come in. Sparx came down a few days later. We had the same set-up, but he was a lot more wary than Fig and didn't stay long, but it went well. Using your dog's natural downtimes for the meetings is really helpful. If these don't occur at a convenient time, take her out for an additional walk or here is where your long-lasting chews can come in handy to keep her calm, happy and occupied when she is around your cat.

Gradual integration

Once your cat is over the initial surprise of sharing the home with a dog, you can gradually increase the amount of time they can spend together. Keep your dog on lead at first to prevent a chase, but you will quickly discover if she is motivated to chase your cat and if she shows no inclination, you can take the lead off, but keep treats and toys to hand to call her back to you if she approaches the cats.

We continued to keep Bucky separate from the cats when we weren't able to supervise, but gradually began to increase the amount of time they spent together and included times when Bucky was awake and active but avoided those when his behaviour was absolutely bonkers. He was soon spending every evening upstairs in the living room with us, meaning the cats could come down into the kitchen if they wanted to. This took a LOT of active management from me and my husband for weeks (and months). You cannot afford to turn your back at this stage, and I spent an endless number of evenings sitting on the floor tirelessly playing tug with Bucky to distract him from going over and sticking his nose in the cat bed where both cats were snuggled up together. Once he did settle, the rest of the evening was very uneventful. We began to get into a routine and things were feeling more normal from just a few weeks in.

A puppy's behaviour will change frequently over the first couple of years as they develop into adults. When Bucky reached adolescence, his behaviour was relentless in the evenings; he would not settle and just wanted to play with us or with the cats. We had a few hissy moments when he would jump into a play bow in front of Fig, who was not impressed with this silliness at all. To work around this, we gave Bucky an extra walk at 6pm to help settle him down for the rest of the evening, which worked really well. These random challenges will present themselves and it can take some thought to work around them without it affecting the budding relationship between your dog and your cat.

The last stage

It took two years before I felt comfortable leaving Bucky unsupervised with Fig and Sparx. In all this time, he had not shown any aggressive behaviour towards them and (other than the occasional hiss if he tried to play with them), they hadn't shown any aggression towards him either. We were always conscious to ensure they had more good experiences together than difficult ones, to build the cats' resilience. They were able to cope better with Bucky's playful behaviour as it happened so infrequently in the grand scheme of the time they spent together. Up until this stage, Bucky had slept downstairs and the cats were up with us, but at two years we finally felt comfortable bringing him upstairs with us at night. His little face when he came up the first night made me feel dreadful for not doing it sooner, but, by this point, the cats were completely comfortable with him and his behaviour was calm and consistent. A year on, and my husband and I continue to share our bed with one Lab, two cats and, more often than not, one, two or three children and we wouldn't change it!

SETTING UP FOR LONG-TERM SUCCESS

This section is also relevant to help you if you already have a dog and a cat that aren't getting along so well. Ideally, your home will already be set up to be very cat friendly, with plenty of resting areas, high places and hiding places, as these will help them share your home happily.

High places

High places will make the biggest difference to their relationship and they enable you to set up your home to work for both animals. Dogs generally prefer to stay at ground level, whereas cats usually gravitate up high, so feeding into this will keep them both happy and help them keep out of each other's way.

Cat trees, furniture and shelving are all ideal for helping your cat to get off the ground and out of your dog's reach. If you have a big dog or a bouncy dog, your cat may need to be up much higher than if you have a small dog. The cat 'perches' need to be easy to get to, so position them in strategic places such as by the entrance to your living room. Your cat may want to feel invisible to your dog and not draw attention to himself, so avoid set-ups where he has to cross the room to the cat tree, as he might find this too daunting. Placing it near the entrance makes it easy for him and will help him feel safer and more in control when your dog is nearby.

Bolt-holes

These are places where your cat can go to hide that your dog cannot get to. If your dog gets too excited and spooks the cat, he needs to know he has somewhere safe to run to. Never block off the exits to a room or his safe spaces as he will feel trapped and will be more likely to panic if he suddenly needs to escape.

Spaces under the bed, behind sofas or inside wardrobes work well for this, as well as cardboard boxes and cat igloo beds. Think about where he chooses to hide and create more places like it if possible, particularly in areas where there is often tension between your cat and your dog.

Avoid forced interaction

Just as with multi-cat households, careful thought should be given to where your cat's and dog's belongings are placed in your home. We want them to be around each other when they want to be, not when they feel forced to be. It may take some time, but find areas for your cat's food, water, litter trays or cat flap that your dog cannot access, so he doesn't have to find a way past her every time he wants to use them.

This can be difficult if your dog is hanging around during your cat's mealtimes, especially if you have a greedy dog like a Labrador. Food is a basic need and if your cat has set mealtimes and nothing in between, this is his only opportunity to eat and he will have no choice but to put himself in this stressful situation each and every day. This won't help their relationship and can lead to stress-related illness and associated behaviour problems.

Litter trays are also an important part of your cat's territory that need to be kept out of your dog's reach. Your dog will naturally want to have a sniff or a dig around in there, and some dogs take a liking to cat poo itself. I have come across some dogs who will follow a cat to the litter tray ready to seize the poo after he's finished. It can make him want to hide away while he poos, and he may go behind the sofa or up on the bed where he can't be watched or disturbed by your dog.

If you have found a good match – and with good management – cats and dogs can live happy lives together and, in some cases, become firm friends. It is amazing to see your hard work pay off!

20

What Your Cat Wants You to Know about Play

Cats are often thought of as an independent animal that doesn't crave much input from people. The reality is, cats love to play, especially when they are younger and there are tons of benefits from taking the time to play with your cat.

HOW CATS PLAY

If you watch your cat play with her toys, you'll see it usually replicates hunting behaviour in both actions and motivations.

Behaviour and body language

The behaviours seen when cats play with toys include stalking, pouncing, chasing, grabbing with paws and biting. She may also roll on her side with a larger toy between her paws and kick hard with her back paws. If this is directed towards your arm, it can be painful.

Cats learn how to hunt and play as kittens, and this can influence how they like to play as they get older. Some prefer to catch things in the air, others chase toys along the floor, some prefer to scoop toys up and fling them around.

When they play together, you will see a lot of chasing, wrestling, grabbing, kicking and biting. It can be worrying to watch them bite each other or bunny kick on their heads and faces. However, this sort of wrestling is all light-hearted during play, with claws remaining sheathed, and there shouldn't be any deliberate injuries unless one or both has had enough and this moves on to more serious aggression.

Their general movements are also different while playing together, they become more 'bouncy'. They may rear up on their back paws and may step or hop forwards or to the side in a playful motion. Generally there should not be any vocalising such as hissing or growling.

Motivation

Hunting tends to involve short bouts of energy throughout the day. So it is useful to look to replicate this where you can and play with your cat in frequent, short play sessions, rather than one long one when you come home from work (although this is better than none at all!).

As with hunting, play is motivated by movement, and they are very attentive to moving objects. This explains why so often when I visit a client's home, they have hundreds of cat toys, but complain that they are left ignored on the floor. These toys are essentially dead prey for your cat.

They aren't interesting anymore and are usually not worth trying to chase.

However, get the toys moving and they suddenly have a new-found love for them. You can see how strong their play drive is when you find your cat frantically trying to hunt your dressing gown cord that's trailing behind you on your way down the stairs.

This also explains why your younger cat prefers to annoy your older cat. Your older cat will be a moving target and will run away when chased. This is much more rewarding and fun than the boring toys on the floor.

It is up to you to motivate your cat to play, merely providing the toys is not enough.

THE BENEFITS OF PLAY

Opportunity for natural behaviours

Every animal needs to have opportunities to perform natural behaviours to ensure their welfare doesn't suffer. This applies to cats as much as other animals, and we take on this responsibility when we invite cats to live in our homes. Remember your cat still retains many of the traits and behaviours of wild cats, so will need something to stalk, chase, pounce on and grab. Without any outlet for these natural behaviours, frustration will soon set in, and you will have problems on your hands. Play provides mental stimulation and enriches their lives and environment to ensure they are behaviourally healthy and well-rounded cats.

Building confidence

Nervous or timid cats are common among the cat population, and I am often asked to help them come out of their shells and bond with their owners. Play is an effective tool for this sort of problem. Once they have found a small amount of confidence to begin playing, this just grows and grows as the cats begin to enjoy themselves, letting go of some of the anxiety they must be experiencing.

Preventing unwanted behaviour

Playing with your cat will pay off for you too. I have heard myself telling owners 'the devil makes work for idle paws' way too often and it is true. Despite having an entire pet shop of toys to play with, cats may prefer to shred the wallpaper and have a blast with the dangling strips, or knock small objects off the mantelpiece and onto the floor because it's fun to see them drop (plus it gets almost immediate attention from us, but that's another problem!). They need to be played with, and it needs to be fun!

Preventing predatory aggression

Predatory aggression (or misdirected play) is a problem I frequently experience with my clients. This can look very scary. They can stalk, pounce on, grab and bite your arms or ankles, just as they would when they are hunting. They aren't actually trying to hunt or hurt you though, this is only play, but can be difficult to manage and very painful. Playing with your cat can help redirect this problem by providing an appropriate outlet for them. All you have to do is make sure the toys are more fun to play with than your ankles!

Many rescues and other organisations recommend homing kittens in pairs so they have a playmate with an equally high play drive. This usually works well to take the heat off the other animals in the home and give your ankles a break. I once worked with a client who was genuinely concerned I would recommend his kitten was put to sleep as his play aggression was so bad and his owner couldn't see how to stop it. Once we talked through the problem and understood the aggression was totally normal (and not really aggression) and he just needed a LOT of playtime, he could breathe a sigh of relief that he was not a bad kitten. However, he worked away from home nine to five, so his kitten was bored when my client was out and he squeezed all of his kitten energy into the time he was home. This wasn't meeting his needs and he found a companion – another young and playful kitten – and they have been firm friends ever since. The aggression stopped almost instantly and he had a willing playmate and company day and night. You must make sure both kittens are equal in temperament for this to be a good move. Pairing a boisterous kitten that is always on the go with one that is more quiet and timid is unlikely to work.

It is important to resolve this sort of problem as early as possible – being stalked and grabbed is not funny and it's much more difficult to stop once they have matured.

Protecting other animals

If you live in a household with another cat or dog and there is a mismatch in play drives because your cat wants to play a lot more than the other animal, problems are not far away. Moving targets are more fun to play with than stationary ones, so if you stop playing, she is going to turn to chasing your other cat, who, of course, runs away, and the game becomes much more fun. It is unfair to allow the other animals in your home to take the brunt of their relentless playfulness and if this is happening, it is time to up your game with playtimes.

Just as we regard walking a dog as an essential part of living with a dog, play sessions with your cat should be considered an essential part of sharing your life with a cat.

HOW TO PLAY WITH YOUR CAT

Clients will often tell me their cat doesn't like to play. If you feel the same, it can help to take time to discover how your cat likes to play and what will get them motivated and keep them entertained.

Keep it moving

We know that moving toys encourage a lot more play than stationary ones. But the way we move the toys can influence this too. Some cats will play with anything that moves, and you'll have no trouble at all finding a toy they love. Others will show a preference for toys that run along the ground, such as a ribbon or stuffed mouse attached to a stick on a length of string so they can stalk, chase and catch it. Others will prefer you to wave these sorts of toys up and above their heads (those with feathers attached work well here) so they can leap up, bat it with their paws and catch it in mid-air. Or your cat may prefer more erratic movement, such as small, coiled springs that bounce along the floor, or toys attached to a length of thin, bouncy wire. It can take some time to find out what they enjoy the most.

You can also move the toys at different speeds to make the toy more enticing. Start a few feet away from them as their eyesight is not so good close-up. Small but sudden movements can catch their eye and give them an opportunity to stalk the toy, before quickly moving it away from them to prompt the chase. Moving the toy under and over different areas can make it more exciting for them too – we have all laughed as our cats jump on the duvet, chasing our feet underneath. With toys, running a mouse on a string under a thin blanket and up and over a cat tree adds some more fun to the game.

Keep it hands-free

It is SO tempting to play with tiny kittens using your fingers and I have been guilty of this in the past before realising what I was doing and stopping myself. They are so small and cute and when you know that tapping your fingers on the ground in front of you like a giant, fleshy spider is almost guaranteed to get their attention, it's next to impossible to resist. And it's cute to see them wrap all four paws around your hand and have a little chew on the end of your finger. Their teeth and claws are almost soft when they are so little and it doesn't hurt, so isn't a problem (you can see where this is going).

However, big problems follow as they get older and I find the most difficult time is around nine to ten months of age when their teeth and claws now mean serious business but they still have all the energy of a bouncy and exuberant kitten. Now, having all four paws surround your arm, furiously bunny kicking, HURTS and makes lots of people upset and even sometimes cross at them.

It's unfair to encourage a behaviour one minute, then scold them for the exact same behaviour the next, just because they're now bigger. This is a man-made problem and takes a lot of input to get them focused on toys and relearn that fingers are not for playing with.

Wand- and fishing-rod-type toys with a long stick can help you keep your hands out of the way from the start and are excellent toys for children to use too, but always supervise when children play with these toys. Alternatively, throwing toys for your cat to chase works well too, and lots of cats like playing fetch games with hair bands or small foam balls (again, supervise!). These hands-off games work so well for cats that are nervous of people. It helps build your relationship with them in a very low-pressure way. They don't need to be near you to enjoy your company.

Roughhousing

Some people tell me (or show me) how they roughhouse with their cat and, honestly, it just makes me cringe. Yes, I'm sure there are cats that genuinely enjoy this sort of interaction (usually a person reaching towards their cat and rolling them over onto their back to rub their tummy). Almost every time this results in the cat grabbing and biting the hand and this response is then likely to happen in other situations, such as the cat launching herself at your hand while you reach for the TV remote. This may not be a problem for you, but, again, it is not fair to expect your cat to know it's OK to bite your hand, but not the hand of child, for example. It also makes me wonder how much the cat is actually enjoying the game or whether the biting is an attempt to get the person to stop. There are lots of better ways to play with your cat that don't have the potential to lead to problems and you know for sure they enjoy.

FINDING THE RIGHT TOYS

Many of the cat toys you see for sale in pet shops and online are made to appeal to us rather than a cat, in terms of the colourful patterns and cute designs. It's understandable, as we are the ones choosing and buying them, and, for the most part, it doesn't take away from the fun (they don't care if it's shaped like a croissant or an avocado – they'll still chase it!). Avoid the temptation to buy whatever looks prettiest and focus on toys that will appeal to a cat. As play is so closely related to hunting, your best bet will be toys that replicate prey in some capacity.

Size

Small, mouse-sized toys are usually played with more than larger toys as they can be easily batted around and manipulated with their paws. Smaller toys usually mean lighter too, so they can also carry them easily in their mouths if the texture allows. This is why they love milk bottle tops; they are so light and easy to bat around on the hard floor of your kitchen (which is usually where they are found).

Your cat may still enjoy playing with larger toys though, particularly the long and thin stuffed shape that they can roll over with and have a good bunny kick.

Sound

Any toy that makes a noise will help get your cat's attention, however, be careful these don't startle her if she is sensitive to sound. Some of the larger bells can be quite loud. Toys that include a crinkly material are good as it can sound like prey rustling nearby, and a high-pitched squeak replicates prey sounds too.

Scent

The most commonly used scent with cat toys is catnip, a mint herb containing the oil nepetalactone, described as a cat attractant. This can cause behavioural changes including rolling over and rubbing against it and they can have a bout of hyperactive behaviour, so it feeds into playtime well and toys infused with catnip are usually played with a lot at first. They may then seem to zone out a little and may lick or chew on a catnip toy.

Some cats can become too overstimulated by catnip and may growl and be more likely to bite while feeling the effects, so use it with care until you know your cat's usual response.

Some are not affected by catnip and show no changes in behaviour. If this is your cat, you can try an alternative such as valerian root, silvervine or Tatarian honeysuckle that can stimulate a similar response to catnip.

Texture

The feel of a toy can make a big difference to how much it is played with. Again, those that share similarities to prey, such as faux fur or feathers, are usually well received, and they can be seen to lick or bite down on these. For this reason, it is good to have a range of toys, including some that are soft and filled with stuffing so she can bite them safely. If it can be ripped open, all the better, although be careful she doesn't ingest any of the toy.

Be careful of textures she may have an aversion to such as pipe cleaners or other potentially spiky or poky parts.

Movement

As we know, cats are stimulated by movement, so think about how a toy moves. Those we move for them are great, the wand types and fishing-rod types, but some toys include other good moving features too. For example, I recently bought my cats a little stuffed spider with eight legs made of thin nylon mesh tubes, with a little weight on the end. The legs bounce around and wiggle everywhere as they play, so it keeps them entertained a lot longer. Think about giving your cat toys that move in various ways, including different sized feathers, small lengths of string, springs and mesh tubes.

Toys that vibrate are good at catching your cat's attention, especially ones that buzz along the floor. But use with care; biting one of these toys would be an unpleasant experience for some.

Novelty

This is one of the most important things to think about when trying to encourage your cat to play. They get bored very quickly playing with the same toy and it won't be long before it becomes part of the furniture, with your cat totally ignoring them as she wanders past. She needs a wide range of different toys, including lots of variations of the factors mentioned above. She may be bored of playing with a stuffed mouse but will be super-keen to play with feathers on a stick. Change the toys during your playtimes to keep them fun and prevent her losing interest. A large collection of cat toys will enable you to give her different ones each day.

Lasers

Cats love chasing lasers and we've all marvelled at their determination to catch that little red dot. There's no doubt that laser pointers are up there as one of the easiest ways to encourage feline play. The fast, unpredictable movement catches their attention and immediately engages the predatory drive. However, they can lead to problems for you and your cat as they don't allow her to finish the hunting sequence in the same way as other toys. She can stalk, chase and pounce on a laser spot, but there is no opportunity to catch or bite it. You risk leaving her in a state of high arousal, hugely motivated to catch this elusive little spot, only to find nothing beneath her paws after a perfectly timed pounce. This can lead to hypervigilant behaviour, over stimulation and frustration, which can easily lead to aggressive behaviour.

I understand how convenient they are and how they generate a high level of play for minimal effort – perfect for those without much time on their hands or with limited mobility. However, lasers should only be used with your cat's behavioural health in mind and in conjunction with different types of toys that she can catch and bite, or try finishing with some food. This will provide an appropriate opportunity to complete the hunting sequence, relieve that frustration and leave her more emotionally stable.

ENCOURAGING INDEPENDENT PLAY

Over recent years, with the onset of COVID and lockdowns, many cat carers have transitioned to home working and it has taken some getting used to, both for us and for our cats. I certainly had a huge influx of clients throughout lockdown, not due to anxiety, as you may expect with everyone at home 24/7, but for those now working from home who could not cope with their cat's attention-seeking behaviour. Constant vocalisation throughout meetings, permanently wandering over laptops and keyboards, even some showing aggression to their owners to get them to turn away from the screen for a moment and show them some attention.

These cats need something to keep them occupied, and, if you are trying to work, you need your cat to entertain herself for a while. Here are some tips on encouraging independent play.

Automatic toys

Movement is a recurring theme throughout this section, so it'll be no surprise to hear that giving your cat moving toys is a great way of stimulating play when you don't have time for play session. As with all toys, it can take some trial and error to find out what works best; some she will love, others, in true, typical cat fashion, will be left totally unused.

Some examples of automatic toys I have seen over the years include a small mouse on a stick that rotates under a small plastic mat; a stuffed fish with a motor inside that flops about on the floor; a plastic ball with a stuffed, fluffy tail attached that rolls erratically around the floor and a small fishing-rod toy attached to a motor that waves the toy around.

Use these toys when you have to, but do not use them to replace regular playtimes. Avoid using them for long periods so she doesn't become frustrated with the lack of downtime.

Food toys

There are plenty of toys and feeders on the market that use food to encourage your cat to play (and it's easy to make your own too!). The simplest and probably most effective type I have found is a hollow plastic ball with multiple holes cut out around the outside. You fill the centre with dry food or treats and your cat uses her nose or paws to roll the ball around and release the treats. This is great for play as she can chase it around and is rewarded with the food as she goes. If you give her regular food in this way, you have changed her mealtimes into a fun and stimulating activity. If you have a cat that needs a lot of stimulation, don't waste mealtimes by feeding from a bowl, it's a lost opportunity.

Other types of feeders encourage different behaviours from your cat. Some require her to pull the food up out of tubes using her paws, or push food down through holes into a container below, and others include mats or boards with grooves or channels that are potentially suitable for wet food too.

It can be fun to create your own cat toys that enable her to rip parts off and find food inside. Small paper parcels of dry food or treats are perfect for this, and you can throw them for your cat to chase. Use toilet roll tubes sealed with cardboard at the ends or egg boxes, anything that you can place a few treats inside and leave for your cat. If you are not so creative, scattering dry food on the grass outside or hiding small piles of dry food around your home provides an opportunity for her to hunt them out.

Play boxes

I love these boxes. It is simply a large, empty cardboard box with different-sized holes cut into the sides and filled with fun things to play with. Lots of different types of toys, plenty of dry food (or a small number of treats) and filled with scrunched-up tissue paper to hide the goodies and give her something to jump or roll around in. You can customise this with the things you know she likes, mine like to hide inside and poke their paws through little holes in the side, but beware sticking your own finger in there, Fig will get you every time.

Remember they love novelty so don't worry if the boxes don't last, see this as an opportunity to change to a new one with different toys and treats inside. If you are not the creative type, you can purchase a double-layer rug with holes in the top layer that does the same thing once you bunch it all up on top of the bottom layer. These are great for kittens, and I recommend them all the time.

Exploring and climbing

As well as playing with toys, your cat may be full of beans and need somewhere to run, jump, and hide in, especially if she is an indoor cat. Tunnels, cat towers and shelving can provide the perfect outlet for this, and you can encourage her to use them by hiding treats and toys up high and in the tunnels for her to find.

21

What Your Cat Wants
You to Know about Moving House

Moving house is a stressful experience for anybody, but it's easy to overlook just how big an impact this has on the cat.

Why it's so stressful

Although cats generally have good relationships with us, they are fiercely territorial and form a strong attachment to their home environment. Their territory is more than just a place for them to live. Their daily routine and activities are focused within their territory, particularly if they have access outside. They can spend hours of their day checking in on their territory, topping up urine marks and keeping an eye on what is happening. Even inside the home will be heavily marked with their familiar and reassuring scent, so removing them from this and placing them in a new home – which is at best a blank slate but at worst smells of other animals – is never going to be an easy task.

Combine this with the stress of the actual move itself, involving carriers, car rides and lots of people and movement, it's easy to see why some cats struggle.

HOW TO REDUCE STRESS

Packing

The packing side of a house move can be super-disruptive to sensitive cats. Some struggle to cope with small changes like rearranging the furniture in your living room, so are going to have a tough time when everything is packed up and ready to go. If you are worried the upheaval will make your cat anxious, you can close him in a different room for a short time while you are packing everything up and let him back out once you have stopped.

Other cats, however, are going to find this a blast. Like mine. We moved house last year and the boys had the best time jumping in and out of empty kitchen cupboards, climbing into half-empty boxes and climbing up the boxes that were packed and sealed. There is no way they would be happy being closed in a separate room and the frustration they would experience from not being part of the action can be just as challenging as the anxiety. So go with your cat. If he behaves like mine, let him explore but keep in mind that once he is ready for a rest and finds you have packed away his favourite bed, this is where he may begin to feel unsettled.

Where possible, store your packed boxes in one room to confine the chaos to a single area and pack his favourite sleeping spots last. Keep any smaller beds or blankets he sleeps on separate from the rest of your belongings as you will need these during the move itself. Try not to dismantle cat trees unless you really need to as these are perfect safe spaces for your cat to use while you are packing everything up.

The big day

If you are able to move over the course of a few days, I would certainly recommend it over moving everything in a single day. If it's not possible, choose a room for your cat to stay while the rest of the house is packed up and carried into the van. This usually involves multiple people doing multiple trips in and out of the house, up and down the stairs, lifting heavy furniture, and they could do without being part of the action and under everyone's feet. The front door is usually left open too and you don't want him creeping out without anyone knowing. Clear this room of the usual furniture before he goes in and place some of his belongings inside, including food, water, litter tray, plenty of beds and blankets, somewhere to hide, somewhere to get up high and his open carrier with comfortable, familiar (not freshly washed) bedding inside. Once the house is packed up and you are ready to leave, place your cat in the carrier and take him separately in your car with you. Pack up the rest of his belongings in a place that will be easy to access once you arrive at your new home, either in the car with you or the last thing to be added to the van. When you arrive, follow the same procedure in reverse. Place all of his belongings in a single room (I would suggest your bedroom so he can sleep with you overnight if you usually let him sleep in your bedroom) and take him to this room before unloading your boxes and furniture for the rest of the house.

When we moved house, I had this planned perfectly for the cats. They were to stay in our bedroom with all their bits and bobs and until the rest of the house was clear and we could move them across. Well, it was a disaster. The removals turned up early and caught me leaving the house for the school run. The cats weren't yet in the bedroom and I wish I had told them to wait but the three men came stomping through the house, in and out of the bedroom. My husband managed to usher the cats into the bathroom just to keep them out of the way. I then spent the whole day stressing about the cats as my plans went out the window at the first hurdle. My point here is – other than being more assertive – try to minimise stress where you can, but keep in mind the day may not go totally to plan, especially if you are moving a long distance and relying on other people who may not see your cat as a big priority.

If you feel your cat won't cope with this amount of upheaval, it is totally fine to place him in a boarding cattery for a few days while you get everything sorted. This can be best case scenario for both you and your cat to avoid such a stressful experience.

Settling in

Your new home will smell totally alien to your cat and he may feel very unsure. You can use scent to help him settle into his new home. His belongings – the things he has slept on or in, and his litter tray – will smell familiar and reassuring. Keep him in a single room for the first day and night to help him relax before exposing him to the rest of the home. This will become his safe space.

The next day (or later if things are not ready or he is taking longer to settle), when your home is calm, open the door and let him explore in his own time. Don't try to encourage him out or pick him up, just give him the option to leave if he wants to. Keep food and litter trays in his room so he leaves the room because he wants to, not because he is looking for food or needs to use a tray.

Move out some (but not all) of his belongings, such as beds and blankets, so he is met with familiar smells as he moves through your home. Pheromone diffusers are helpful here too, to help him feel less anxious and more comfortable while he explores.

For us, Sparx didn't emerge from our bedroom for a few hours, whereas Fig came straight out as soon as the door was opened as he is more confident and sociable – and he wants to be where the people are. I wasn't worried as Sparx was his usual snuggly, purry self with us the night before and when we went up there to see him and he came out when he was ready.

Be mindful of parts of your new home your cat may find more stressful than others. Fig and Sparx quickly settled into the living area as we spent a lot of time there and it was pretty much business as usual quite quickly, with familiar furniture and normal human activities. However, the conservatory was much more of a challenge for them. It is floor-to-ceiling glass on three walls and the outside space is larger than our previous home. This can be both intimidating and overwhelming, particularly as we didn't have one before. It took a couple of weeks for them to feel confident to go in there, but they made their way there when they were ready and now it's a firm favourite spot for them both, especially on sunny days.

Letting them outside

If your cat is used to having free access outside, chances are he will be keen to get out and establish his new territory. It is a good idea to keep him inside your new home for at least two weeks to make sure he has settled in and considers your home his new territory and will come back. If you live relatively near your old home, you risk your cat picking up on his old routes and making his way back to his previous territory, so you may wish to keep him in for longer.

When the time comes:

- Let him explore at his own pace. Avoid carrying him outside or back in if possible.
- Keep the door open the first few times so he has an easy escape route back inside if he gets spooked.
- Keep anything potentially stressful out of the way – my children and my dog stayed inside at first.
- Stay with him to reassure him and keep an eye on where he is going.
- Keep it short at first and let him out just before he is usually fed so he is keen to come back in (or use some treats).

Fig is more outdoorsy than Sparx and he had an explore outside after a few weeks while I had a cup of tea in the garden (it was January, so I was loaded with blankets and a hot water bottle too!). Sparx is more homely than Fig and after around six months, the weather finally warmed up – he is 100 per cent a fair-weather cat – and he finally headed out to enjoy the sunshine. Even after such a long time, he was still tentative, but he found his confidence quickly as he did it all on his own terms. If I had rushed him, I risked making him anxious and causing him to lose his confidence.

Despite all the potential challenges involved with moving house, most cats appear to cope with this huge event surprisingly well. They soon establish a new territory and settle relatively quickly. Another example of how well cats have adapted to a human lifestyle – they never fail to amaze me!

22

What Your Cat Wants You to Know about Catteries and Cat Sitters

Knowing what to do with your cat while you are on holiday is something I struggle to find the perfect answer to. It really depends on your unique circumstances and your unique cat (which is a running theme throughout this book!).

Don't leave her alone

It used to be common for cats to be left to their own devices while their owner was on holiday, with a huge bowl full of dry food and enough water to last until they came home. However, this is not recommended due to the risks your cat may encounter while she is alone. If she falls unwell, there will be no one to help her. Not to mention the mental toll of being left alone for such a long period of time, especially for single cats or those with no access outside. If your cat is able to go outside, there may be risks here too, or she may find her way into a neighbour's house for a bit of company.

CATTERIES AND CAT SITTERS

The most popular alternatives are cat sitters and boarding catteries. Each have their good and bad points and will be suited to some cats but not others.

Cat sitters allow your cat to stay at home, with someone checking in on her morning and evening to give her food, attention and scoop the trays. Catteries require you to take your cat to a boarding establishment where she will be securely housed, usually in a pen, until you return. The territorial nature of a cat makes me feel that keeping her at home in her familiar environment is generally the best option, but there are circumstances where a cattery may be best.

Which one works for you and your cat?

There are no hard-and-fast rules, but you should give thought to how your cat will cope in each situation. Here are some things to consider:

- If you have an independent, outdoorsy cat who comes and goes and does her own thing, a cat sitter would undoubtedly be best. Most of her usual routine can remain the same and she will avoid the frustration of being cooped up in a cattery for long periods of time.
- If your cat stays exclusively indoors and is a single cat, she may become bored and lonely at home without you.

- If your cat is older, she may be more comfortable in her usual sleeping spots, but if she is unwell, she may need to be boarded so someone can keep a closer eye on her.
- If she is stressed by car travel, you can avoid the journey by using a cat sitter.
- If you have more than one cat, they can be good company for each other at home with a cat sitter. But if your cats don't usually get along, it is best to use a cattery and house them in separate pens to avoid any fighting while you are away.
- A cat sitter is usually more affordable than a cattery stay, particularly if you have more than one cat.

What makes a good cat sitter:

- If it is a friend or family member, they must be reliable and trustworthy. You don't want your cat getting forgotten about in the hubbub of everyday life. It will be useful if they know your cat well and they already have a good relationship.
- If you are using a professional cat sitter, they must have insurance.
- A professional should also have references and a proven history of taking good care of cats they look after.
- Your sitter should be knowledgeable about cats, know how to interact with her and understand her behaviour and body language.
- They should know what to do in an emergency and, at the very least, be able to get your cat to a vet

quickly. Vet nurses make fantastic cat sitters as they are usually animal lovers, will be able to administer medication and will know how to help your cat in an emergency.

- They should be mindful of your specific cat's needs and behaviours.

What makes a good cattery:

- With so many cats in one place, disease control needs to be priority and it should be a requirement that all cats are appropriately vaccinated. There should be impermeable barriers between pens and no mixing of cats. If there is a communal exercise area where cats spend time together, avoid this cattery.
- The pens should be temperature controlled, particularly when they are in a standalone unit such as a building at the bottom of the cattery owner's garden.
- Noise should be controlled. If the cattery houses dogs too in nearby kennels, they should not be anywhere near the cats to avoid them feeling stressed by any barking.
- The pens themselves should be suitably enriched, including a place to hide (which is essential for stress relief), a place to get up high, toys to play with and a suitable litter tray positioned away from her food and water.
- You should have the option to bring familiar items from home to transfer the scent of home to the pen, and for her to be fed her usual diet.

- Water should be constantly available.
- All staff at the cattery should be knowledgeable about cats, know how to interact with them and understand their behaviour and body language.
- You should be able to choose whether your cats are housed together or apart, based on their relationship at home.
- You should be allowed to visit and see inside the pens to check for yourself you are happy with the facilities they provide. Ask questions and make sure you are satisfied with the answers before agreeing to take your cat here.

I have come down on the side of cat sitters here, though I do wonder whether either option is best for our cats. Home boarders are people that will live in your home for the duration of your holiday. If your cat is friendly with people, and if the person is good with cats, this can work better than a cat sitter in terms of sticking to their usual routine and keeping a close eye on them.

An alternative to catteries is cat hotels. I visited a lady who runs a cat hotel near me recently and was super-impressed. Four of her bedrooms were dedicated cat rooms – very comfortable, cat-friendly rooms, full of places to sleep, climb, hide, play and even a single bed with a duvet and pillows. Each room had CCTV for the cat's carer to check in on 24/7 and she was able to spend lots of her time with each of them as she only boarded four cat families at once and there was plenty of space in the rooms for her to be in with them too.

There is no right or wrong answer here, give it due thought, but do what works best for you and your cat.

23

What Your Cat Wants You to Know about Behaviour Problems

In my role as a cat behaviour counsellor, I have seen hundreds, if not thousands of cats who are displaying challenging behaviours. The interesting thing about this is that what we consider to be a behaviour problem usually isn't a problem at all for your cat – it is a very reasonable and understandable response to the current situation he finds himself in. And with almost every single cat I have worked with, we have been able to unpick the problem to find out what initially caused the behaviour and what is stopping it from improving.

For example, would you pee in a toilet that hasn't been cleaned or flushed for a week? I wouldn't. Not happily anyway. So, it is perfectly reasonable for your cat to find another place to go where he feels more comfortable. This is a classic example of a cat developing a problem behaviour because their needs are not being adequately met.

Treating feline behaviour problems is not about forcing a cat to accept the challenges of a human lifestyle. It involves understanding what your cat needs (physically and emotionally) and making changes to your own behaviour or environment to help him feel happier and more comfortable. A suitably qualified and experienced cat behaviourist can help you resolve this issue so you no longer have to go on a hunt for pee every morning when you wake up and your cat can relax in a home where they have everything they need.

The difficult part is working out what it is they need. Every cat is different. They are a product of their experience, both through their socialisation and through the experiences they have had throughout their lives.

COMMON BEHAVIOURAL PROBLEMS

Below are the most common behaviour problems I am asked to help with. If you are experiencing any of these problems, you may find some of the advice here helpful, especially if the problem has only just started. Remember to ask your vet to check for any medical factors first and ask for a referral to a cat behaviourist if you aren't making any progress.

Toileting in unwanted places

This is where your cat may pee or poo in areas of your home where you do not intend them to go. Common areas include on beds, sofas, carpets, rugs and bathtubs, but it could be anywhere. Because we are talking about an elimination behaviour, your cat will usually squat down and leave a puddle of wee on the surface below. This is different to marking behaviour where the pee is sprayed onto a vertical surface (see Urine-marking).

As long as your cat is healthy, this problem is usually due to issues around their designated toileting areas or problems getting to them. If your cat finds your home a stressful environment, she may not feel comfortable travelling to the cat flap or litter tray. She may not be comfortable using the type of litter or shape and size of the litter tray itself. Some cats have developed a preference for the type of material they pee on, such as carpet or soft furnishings.

Urine-marking

When a cat sprays urine onto a vertical surface, it's not because they need to pee but because they want to mark their territory. If they start doing this indoors, it usually indicates they feel their territory is not safe, which could be due to sources of stress both inside or outside your home. Changes to the home such as redecorating or renovations can trigger this problem, as well as people leaving or joining the household. Probably the biggest cause of this issue is conflict with other cats in your home or new cats intimidating your cat outside.

Some cats urine-mark when they are frustrated, such as when they are prevented from going outside at certain times or when they are expecting food and it doesn't arrive. Urine-marking is a very complicated problem, often with lots of emotions at play.

Aggression to people

Your cat may display aggressive behaviour towards you in the form of swiping, biting, grabbing, kicking with her back paws, hissing, growling or spitting. Petting aggression is when this behaviour is triggered by you stroking her in a way she is not comfortable with. Most people say this behaviour comes out of nowhere, but often she will give subtle hints that she is becoming less tolerant of being stroked and wants it to stop.

Predatory aggression is usually misdirected play or hunting behaviour rather than them trying to hurt you. As they are sensitive to movement, they are driven to chase and catch moving objects such as hands and ankles – and feet under the duvet are the best thing ever to chase and catch.

If your cat is displaying serious aggression with loud vocalisations such as yowling or caterwauling, get yourself away immediately. Isolate her and give her time to calm down, before finding help from a professional cat behaviourist. Cat bites and scratches can be very serious and can quickly become infected, particularly for young children and older people.

Aggression to cats

There are a LOT of cats in the world. Most are living either with at least one other cat in their home, and/or in the surrounding area. This can lead to rising tensions and conflict is almost unavoidable in some areas where the feline population is high.

Cats that live together will often display more low-level aggression than unfamiliar cats. There may be some chasing and fighting, but often the fights do not result in injury. There are more subtle behaviours such as blocking access to resources and intense staring, and the constant challenge of trying to navigate this without fighting can induce chronic stress.

Cat fights outside are a lot more serious, as you may have witnessed or, worse, experienced with your own cat. Long stare offs often result in a very tense fight and, in my experience, abscesses and injuries are more common between unfamiliar cats fighting in their overlapping territory. If your cats are fighting to this extent inside your home it is a serious matter, and you need behavioural help ASAP.

Overgrooming

This is an issue that is too often considered a behaviour problem when, in my experience, most cases of cats grooming excessively is due to an underlying physical cause. By all means, remove anything your cat clearly finds stressful, but often people presume it is purely behavioural and stop any further medical investigations. Your vet needs to rule out allergies, skin conditions, internal pain and discomfort, and urinary issues as a minimum, and I'm sure there are plenty more potential medical causes I am missing.

Excessive vocalisation

This may not seem like a big problem, but if you are living with a cat that wakes you up from vocalising at all hours of the night or at the crack of dawn every morning, you will appreciate just how much of an impact this can have on your life and your mental health. I frequently receive emails at 3, 4 or 5am from desperate people who just cannot take another night of no sleep. They will do this at other times of the day too, and it is hard not to worry that they are in pain or that they need something they aren't getting, such as food or attention. It's a difficult problem to crack because of how much we care for them.

VETERINARY EXAMINATION

If your cat is showing a problem behaviour, the first thing to do is talk to your vet about it, particularly if her behaviour is out of character. The reason for this is that any behaviour can be caused or exacerbated by a medical factor – literally any. So even if you feel that the cause of the problem is obvious – perhaps you have brought home a new cat and they are not getting along; she may be less tolerant to the new cat as she is not feeling 100 per cent. We need to have all the information to be able to appropriately treat the problem while not compromising on her welfare.

Your vet should give your cat a thorough examination and depending on the issue, may decide to do some further tests. Urinary issues are common in cats, which can lead them to avoid the litter tray if it's painful to pee, so running a urine test is good practice to rule this out first. Dental issues are common too and a couple of years ago I worked with a little cat who wasn't getting along with the new dog. Her vet found she needed ten teeth out and once she had recovered, she was a lot more easygoing and accommodating of the dog's behaviour.

On the flip side, keep in mind that your vet cannot possibly rule out all potential medical causes on the first examination. So, it is important your vet, your behaviourist and you work as a team to get to the bottom of the problem and cover all bases to maximise your cat's well-being and give you the best chance of resolving the problem.

THE ROLE OF EMOTIONS

Of course, it is not just physical health that can influence behaviour, your cat's emotional well-being plays an important part too. Cats are sensitive beings, capable of experiencing a wide range of emotions such as happiness and contentment, as well as more negative emotions such as anxiety, fear or frustration, and these can manifest into behaviour problems. For example, if your cat is feeling anxious about the scary cat that's moved in next door, it may prompt them to urine-mark to provide a reassuring sign within the territory.

It is generally believed that cats are not capable of experiencing more complex emotions such as guilt, spite or jealousy. I find this so interesting as so many clients will use these emotions to describe how their cat is feeling when explaining their behaviour. For example, I often hear them referring to 'protest pees' when their cat pees on the bed when the client is on holiday or believing their cat is behaving aggressively to their new partner out of jealousy.

This highlights how misunderstood cats often are, and these interpretations of their feelings can affect how a person feels and acts towards them. If you believe your cat is peeing on your bed out of spite, you are more likely to be cross at them for it. But if you think of them as feeling anxious when they are left alone and peeing in a comforting location, it is much easier to empathise with them and look to understand how to make them feel better in this situation. The problem will be much easier to resolve if we keep this mindset.

Stress

Stress is a physical and emotional response to an environmental threat or difficult situation. Their 'fight or flight' systems are activated, and, in a fearful situation, this response can help them to survive – such as prompting them to run away when a dog approaches. In many cases, the stress response is activated in a situation where a cat cannot escape, leading them to experience chronic stress. This can severely impact their health and behaviour and you may notice them becoming more withdrawn, less sociable, hiding more, losing their appetite, toileting in unwanted places and potentially over-grooming.

Common causes of chronic stress can include a poor environment, unwanted interactions from the people in the home and other animals inside and outside the home. Anything can be a potential source of stress for your cat, as they are all individuals and what they find threatening may be different to what another cat finds threatening. Bear in mind, they only need to THINK it is something to worry about, even if it wouldn't actually cause them any harm.

Interplay between physical and emotional health

Physical health and emotional health often go hand in hand. If you are feeling physically unwell, your emotional state is likely to be low too. And likewise, if you are feeling stressed, this will affect your body's ability to cope with physical illness and will affect the functioning of your immune system. The same can be said for cats.

A practical example of this is commonly seen in cats suffering from feline idiopathic cystitis (FIC – a painful urinary condition), which is commonly exacerbated by stress. A potential symptom of FIC is peeing in unwanted places, most likely because passing urine becomes painful so they may not feel comfortable using a tray. The pain induces further stress, and the cycle continues, leading to a deterioration in both your cat's physical and emotional well-being and potentially affecting their welfare.

THE ROLE OF LEARNING

Learnt behaviours are problems that may have started for one reason, but were subsequently reinforced by a desired outcome, leading the behaviour to continue even once the original cause has been resolved. Here's an example from my own cat – Sparx. He loves sleeping on my youngest daughter's bed throughout the day (she has the squashiest duvet) but her door is closed at night. One night when she was two years old, Sparx tried scratching at her door, presumably with the intention of opening the door to access his favourite sleeping place. Anyone with a toddler will know how precious sleep is (to me at least!) and on hearing him scratching, I leapt out of bed at top speed and coaxed him into my bed where he purred away happily while I lavished him with attention to get him to settle down. You can see where this is going. Every night after that, he would scratch at her door in the night, not with the original intention of getting in, but with the much bigger reward of me being wide awake and him becoming the centre of my world for a bit. And even with the foresight of knowing I was making a rod for my own back, I still leapt up to get him, too worried by the thought of him waking my daughter.

It is so easy to accidentally reinforce your cat's tricky behaviours but is much more difficult – and takes a long time – to undo them. In the end, I was barricading my daughter's door with pillows at night and I made Sparx his own squashy mini duvet bed on the side of my bed

266

before he was finally happy to settle down without going through the usual scratching routine, but it took weeks. As well as thinking about the original cause of a problem behaviour, take time to think about what the consequences are too.

MULTIPLE CAUSES

As you may have grasped through this chapter so far, there is usually a complicated mix of causes and contributing factors to a single behaviour problem. This explains why generic advice is so difficult to apply to your unique cat once the problem has become well established.

Take an aggressive cat. She may be being aggressive because she is getting older and is experiencing the onset of osteoarthritis, meaning her joints are becoming more stiff and painful (physical factor). Because of this, it hurts when she is picked up and she becomes anxious when she thinks it might happen. She starts feeling on edge around her owner in case it happens (emotional factor). When she is picked up, she responds aggressively as she is already distressed from the anxiety and she is experiencing physical discomfort too, so she responds with a hiss and a bite. She is quickly placed back down so the hissing and biting becomes a learnt behaviour too, as the aggression led to the desired consequence of being left alone.

This is now a very complicated problem, and will require much time and thought to unpick and address all of the factors at play.

FIND HELP SOONER RATHER
THAN LATER

If you are experiencing a problem with your cat's behaviour, if you can, get help right away. As we know, there could be a medical cause that needs treating or an emotional issue affecting her well-being. Please don't leave it. It isn't fair on your cat, and it isn't fair on you either. You don't have to live with your cat peeing up the walls. It isn't normal for your cat to bite and scratch you on a daily basis. It's stressful for your cat to live a constantly hypervigilant life in case they cross paths with your other cat.

The sooner you find help the better and the easier it will be to resolve. I have worked with owners whose cats have been urine-marking for years and years, and it is almost impossible to totally stop a problem that has become so ingrained.

I have also worked with clients who are in tears at how much of their life is taken up by living around their cat's problem behaviours. They are worried the house smells like pee, they are reluctant to invite friends into their home in case they are scratched, they are worried about their cat's being unhappy, but just don't know what to do about it. If this sounds like you, you don't have to live this way, help is out there.

POTENTIAL SOLUTIONS

Once a problem has become well established, generic advice usually isn't enough to resolve the issue. Most behaviour problems require a unique and detailed plan to resolve the problem for that specific cat, in that specific situation. However, I don't think I have seen a client who hasn't already tried to stop the problem themselves by searching for advice online, in books and from friends. And sometimes, particularly if the problem has just started, a small change can make a big difference. Here are some things to consider when looking to stop your cat's challenging behaviour:

Consult your vet

The behaviour is unlikely to stop if there is a medical problem left untreated.

Punishment

It is not OK to punish your cat for her annoying behaviours. Shouting, smacking, water sprays, hissing air canisters, rattle cans or any other device intended to scare your cat off will not be good for her or your relationship with her. Trust me, it is a recipe for disaster, and here's why:

1. Your relationship with your cat is built on trust. They are not originally a social species; they don't have that inherent biological need to be part of a social group. If she no longer trusts you, she may not want to be around you.

2. For punishment to work, it must be scary, painful or unpleasant. We know just how many problems can be caused by fear and anxiety, so you risk causing more problems than you solve.

3. You risk making the problem a lot worse, particularly with toileting issues and aggression issues. A few years ago, I worked with a lady and her fluffy ginger cat. He would bite her if she stroked him for too long, so she would smack him on the nose. He started to pre-empt a smack by hissing at her before she even began stroking him and the aggression got much worse with him attacking her before she actually did anything to him.

4. If punishment works, this essentially just sticks a plaster over the problem. You need to find out the root cause of why they are acting out – they need empathy, not punishment. This takes time, I know it's not a quick fix, but there's a reason for it and we owe it to them to take the time to find out what it is.

Make sure you are meeting your cat's needs

The International Society of Feline Medicine (ISFM) and American Association of Feline Practitioners (AAFP) created five pillars of a healthy feline environment. It can help eliminate behaviour problems and increase your cat's well-being to ensure each of the five pillars are in place.

1. Provide a safe space

As cats do not rely on other animals for survival (such as lions that hunt in prides), they need to keep themselves safe, and feel a lot more comfortable with reliable access to a safe space. Your home itself should be a safe place for your cat, so identify anything she may find potentially stressful and remove this if you can.

If it is not possible to remove sources of stress, manage them where you can to reduce the impact on your cat. For example, if you are redecorating, do this one room at a time so she has plenty of unchanged areas to spend time in.

As well as removing stress-inducing stimuli, it is also important to include additional areas within your home to help her feel safer. For example, adding plenty of high places will allow her to keep an eye on the territory while feeling confident and out of harm's way. Cardboard boxes (and other hiding places) provide a feeling of security too, so they need plenty of these, in various areas throughout your home. Position both hiding places and high places in areas where they may feel less confident, such as near windows or busy areas, as well as in the places where they like to spend much of their time.

2. Provide multiple and separate key environmental resources

This is touching on what I have covered already and is most important in a multi-cat household. Every cat should be able to access their resources freely (food, water, toileting areas, scratch posts, toys, beds and perches), so these should be positioned in convenient and easily accessible areas and away from anything scary. They should be positioned separately so that in a multi-cat household the cats have the choice to avoid each other and are not forced to congregate around a resource if they want to use one at the same time. Remember the rule of one per cat, plus one (but way more beds and high places than that!).

3. Provide opportunity for play and predatory behaviour

The ability to display natural behaviours is essential for any animal's welfare and predatory behaviour is one that is crucial for your cat, particularly when she is younger. Engaging her in fun and enthusiastic play sessions will help to encourage this (remember you will need to make the toys move to encourage her to play), as well as placing her food in an activity feeder. Cats that have access outside are less likely to need you to play with them as frequently as an indoor cat, as they can perform so much more natural behaviour in a suitable outside space.

4. Provide positive, consistent and predictable human-cat social interaction

Most cats will form positive relationships with people, but the interactions need to be handled in a way that your cat is OK with. Her tolerance to petting and being picked up will vary, so you must make sure the way you behave towards your cat is a way that suits her. She must feel in control so always offer your hand towards her to see if she wants to interact and only stroke her for short periods, with breaks in between.

Punishing your cat by shouting at her will make you unpredictable and this is unsettling. Another reason why it is so important not to use punitive methods to treat behaviour problems.

5. Provide an environment that respects the importance of the cat's sense of smell

Your cat defines her territory through smell and scent-marking which helps her feel secure and comfortable. Allow her to scent-mark by facial-marking or body-rubbing and provide plenty of scratch posts to allow her to mark through scratching too. Take care not to remove the invisible marks left behind through cleaning or redecorating.

Avoid wearing strong perfume, using strong air fresheners or using any scented cat litter.

You can use synthetic pheromones to help your cat feel safer and more secure within her territory.

To eliminate behaviour problems, you need to understand your unique cat's needs, based on her temperament, experiences and the environment in which she find herself in. Look at your home from her perspective, and try to understand why she is behaving this way. This is difficult when you are very attached to your cat or if you have lived with her problem behaviour for a long time, so it can help to call in a professional to help you break down and understand the problem by looking at her behaviour from an independent perspective.

REHOMING

As a final note here, it is not a failure if you feel you need to rehome your cat because you are unable to resolve her behaviour. If you know she is unhappy, this is one of the biggest kindnesses you can offer her. I once worked with a cat who urine-marked up to fifteen times a day, all along the inside of the back of his house, including the kitchen and conservatory that faced into the back garden. Outside were tons of unfamiliar cats – some just passing through, others hanging around a lot more, intimidating my client's cat all day long. There was nothing she could do to keep these cats away. The garden was surrounded by other gardens, the fences were only four-foot high, finances prevented her from enclosing the garden and even if she did, these cats would still be able to see in. This little cat was spending all of his time worrying about the other cats outside; his home did not feel safe, and he was not enjoying his life constantly feeling his home was at risk and needed defending. We found him a new home and there was an instant change. The environment was completely different, with a wide-open space outside and fewer cats around. He could breathe a sigh of relief to no longer have to worry, so, although it was sad to see him go, this was the best thing for him.

What can make me sad is a well-meaning person who point-blank refuses to consider rehoming under any circumstances. I know this is coming from a good place, and they feel as though they would never want to see their cat go through the experience of going into a shelter. Or they are worried about passing a problem on, or feeling as though they are giving up on their beloved cat (or more commonly, all of the above), but it keeps me up at night knowing cats I have worked with are so miserable and will never be out of that situation. I will always do everything I can to help keep a cat in their home, but sometimes, it really is the best thing you can do. Though it is never easy.

24

What Your Cat Wants You to Know about Veterinary Care

We all want our cats to live long and healthy lives with minimal veterinary intervention. However, this is a difficult area with cats as they are biologically primed to hide any indicators of pain. This comes back to the cat essentially being a prey species (as well as a predator) – any obvious display of weakness will highlight them as an easy target to potential predators. This is such a difficult part of cat ownership as we never really know what they are experiencing or how they are feeling. It is a sad realisation that once physical problems are bad enough to significantly affect your cat's behaviour, they are very bad indeed. This assumed resilience to painful conditions can skew our belief that medication is necessary. For example, I have known many cats that are not given any pain relief to take home following their neuter or spay operation, despite the procedures being painful for several days afterwards, particulary for females. No one would choose to leave their cat in pain, but a natural bias comes into play here. We inherently want them to be healthy and to not require any veterinary intervention, and their apparent normal behaviour supports that bias. We really need to consider the situation objectively and advocate for our cats as, after all, leaving them to suffer in silence is a welfare concern, whether we mean it to happen or not.

Cats experience pain to the same degree as any other species and to give them the best life possible we need to be proactive in keeping on top of their health and well-being. So regular check-ups with a cat-friendly vet are essential, particularly when he is older or if he has an existing health condition. Your vet will be able to pick up on any potential concerns and work on treating the problem as early as possible. Some problems are more common than others, including kidney disease and dental problems that, again, can go unnoticed for a long time before obvious symptoms arise. Osteoarthritis is another condition common in older cats and if I am working with an older cat, I always presume they have some degree of joint pain or stiffness and tailor my advice to cater for the needs of an ageing cat. I understand veterinary intervention has financial implications and, in my opinion, pet insurance is an essential part of cat ownership. Take out the best cover you can afford or keep a reserve of money aside for your cat's vet bills if you prefer to do this instead. If you cannot afford your cat's veterinary care and are concerned he is unwell, there are charities that can help you. Cats are not low-maintenance animals, please don't leave them untreated.

PREVENTATIVE HEALTHCARE

Neutering

Neutering will bring significant health benefits, particularly if undertaken early. It will protect your female cat from the risks of pregnancy, false pregnancy and the pain and aggression involved with mating. She will have a reduced risk of cancer and uterus infections too. Your male cat will be protected from testosterone-driven fights with other males and the dangers of roaming far and wide in search of females while also eliminating the risk of testicular cancer.

Vaccinations

Vaccinations are an essential part of cat ownership that are vital in preventing your cat or kitten falling seriously unwell, especially if they are very young, very old or have another health condition. Vaccinations also prevent the spread of disease among other cats, which is important in areas where there is a high population of free-living cats where few may be vaccinated themselves. Feline Leukaemia Virus is spread through the saliva of other cats and cat flu is highly contagious and can seriously affect the health of your cat or kitten and can even be fatal.

It is recommended that indoor cats are vaccinated, as well as those with access outside. This is because some diseases (such as feline parvovirus) can be easily walked into homes on shoes or clothing, and there is always the risk your indoor cat will accidentally find themselves outside. It is recommended that kittens are vaccinated around eight or nine weeks, and again four weeks later, so your kitten's breeder should be taking care of this first part for you, and boosters will be required throughout their lives. If your adult cat is not currently vaccinated, you can start this process at any time.

Parasite treatment

Fleas cause an unpleasant itching which can cause excessive scratching or biting at the skin, leaving sore patches. Flea allergies are fairly common, where the skin can become inflamed and scabby, leading to loss of fur from the increased scratching on irritated skin. It must be very uncomfortable for them. Fleas can jump onto your cat when they are outside in grassy areas, but indoor cats can catch them too. They can be brought inside your home from other animals that do go outside such as your dog, and although fleas do not survive on people, they can be carried on clothing. Once fleas have a chance to breed inside your home and you have an infestation on your hands, it is a massive job to get rid of them.

Worms are a common parasite that live inside a cat's body rather than on their skin. Roundworm and tapeworm are the most common in the UK. It can be very serious – possibly life-threatening for kittens as it can prevent them absorbing the required nutrients from their food and can damage the inside of the intestines. These parasites can be carried by fleas, caught from eating prey items such as birds or rodents, or, sadly, can be caught from their mother's milk as a kitten.

If your cat is not currently protected, there are some very effective spot treatments for both fleas and worms available from your vet that are applied to the back of your cat's neck. This will kill the worms but will only remove the fleas living on your cat, so if you already have an infestation, you will need to treat the carpets and furniture in your home too. Only a small percentage of fleas are actually on your cat once an infestation breaks out, the majority live in your home and eggs can lie dormant for a long time before they are disturbed and go on to hatch. Prevention is better than cure in this situation, so keep up with your flea and worming treatments.

HOW TO TELL IF YOUR CAT IS UNWELL

As we know, cats don't make it obvious when they are experiencing any pain or discomfort. But there are some behavioural indicators that ring alarm bells when you know what to look for. The overarching takeaway from this section is – know what is normal for your cat. Be aware of any changes and check them out with your vet.

Body language

If your cat has been injured, you will notice if they are limping or have accumulated any obvious wounds, but it is more tricky when the problem is internal or more of a slow deterioration such as dental pain. Some signs to look for include:

- Crouching or sitting hunched over with their head held lower than their shoulders;
- Ears slightly flattened and rotated so you can see part of the back of the ear from the front;
- Eyes squinted or closed for long periods of time;
- Tight muzzle area with whiskers straight and pushed forward.

Sorry, I did say it was subtle!

Behaviour

Identifying changes in your cat's behaviour can be more straightforward and the key is to check out any behaviours that are unusual for your cat, with your vet. Some common behavioural signs of pain are listed below. You will notice some of them can manifest in problem behaviours that I am often asked to help my clients with. This is why I will only ever see a cat once they have been checked over by their vet, so we can be sure there are no medical conditions causing the problem or if there are, these can be appropriately treated or managed before we move on to behavioural treatment:

- **Increased irritability** – Your cat's temperament may appear to change in that he is less tolerant to being touched or picked up and may respond with aggression. He may be less accommodating of other pets in the household too and may begin to avoid them.

- **Excessive hiding** – Your cat may just want to take himself away and stop interacting with the environment as he would have previously. Only coming out for food, water and to use the litter tray is not a sign of a happy, healthy cat.

- **Increased sleeping** – Your cat may stop enjoying the activities he used to like such as spending time outside, approaching you for social interaction or playing with toys. Yes, this could be a natural part of getting older, but that doesn't mean his pain or discomfort should be ignored and labelled as consistent with age.

- **Reduced mobility** – You may notice your cat is no longer able to jump up onto the kitchen worktops or comfortably move through the cat flap. If he is hesitating before making a jump rather than doing so quickly and freely, there is a good chance he is finding it painful.

- **Changes in grooming** – If cats are in pain, it may become more difficult for them to keep up with grooming their coat, particularly in hard-to-reach areas such as around the back end. You may notice his fur becomes matted and unkempt. Also keep an eye out for too much grooming, which can be an attempt to ease discomfort. For example, it is common for cats experiencing urinary tract infections to excessively lick their abdomen and the inside of their back legs, sometimes leaving bald patches.

- **Changes in eating or drinking habits** – Consistently eating or drinking more or less than usual can be an indication that something is not right, just like Fig's increase in water intake which led to his diabetes diagnosis.
- **Changes in toileting habits** – As urinary tract infections are common among cats, they can associate litter trays with painful urination and look for more comfortable places to go. If they usually pee and poo outside, any form of pain or discomfort will make it more challenging for them to make their way out. Some conditions may cause them to pee more frequently so any changes need to be discussed with your vet.

REDUCING STRESS AT THE VETS

Taking a cat to the vet's is a notoriously difficult task for many people. As cats are happiest when they are in control of their own behaviour and environment, a trip to the vet involves a total loss of control and plenty of stressors. Being confined to a carrier, travelling in a noisy vehicle, encountering other animals in a clinic that smells totally alien and being restrained and handled uncomfortably during an examination are all stressful experiences of a typical visit to the clinic. If your cat is already unwell, such stress risks exacerbating the condition and affecting his treatment. Here are some ways you can help keep stress to a minimum when taking your cat to the vet.

Carrier training

For the most part, we don't take cats out of the house in the same way we do dogs. Generally, most dogs leave the house for a good reason, they love going for walks and joining their owners in cafes and on holidays. Perhaps one in one hundred trips out may be for a vet visit for a healthy dog. Whereas for a cat, almost every time they are placed in a carrier, it is to go somewhere unpleasant. No wonder so many disappear the moment you bring the carrier in from the garage. One piece of advice here – take your cat to the carrier, not the carrier to your cat to avoid him getting spooked before you have restrained him. It is a challenging situation for both you and your cat when your appointment is imminent and all you can see is a pair of eyes staring back at you from under the bed. This can lead people to panic and resort to desperate measures of pulling them out and forcing them into the carrier. Some tell me they've been in tears themselves, but just didn't know what else to do. This scenario means you and your cat are stressed at the very first step of the process and this is completely avoidable with some forward planning.

Training your cat to feel comfortable in the carrier and to walk in by himself will make both your lives easier and help the appointment go a lot more smoothly. It is the single biggest thing you can do to support your cat (and your vet) in this situation. Here is how you do it:

- Choose a carrier that is large enough for your cat to turn around inside and with a detachable top half. Never place two adult cats together in the same carrier, so if you have more than one cat, they will need a carrier each.
- Permanently leave the carrier out with comfortable bedding inside. Yes, they are bulky, and don't match anyone's decor, but by doing this, you are creating a portable safe space for your cat. If he is already afraid of the carrier, you may need to remove the top part at first and reattach it once he is going in consistently.
- Sporadically place treats inside the carrier for him to find as he investigates. Use his favourite treats so he is keen to follow them into the carrier. At first, don't close him inside, just let him go in and out as he pleases, this way there is no pressure for him to do anything this early on.
- Continue to use the treats to help him become familiar with the carrier. Once he is going in and out happily, you can briefly close the door for a moment to familiarise him with the feeling of being confined. There is no need to do this for long periods at home.
- When the time comes for the appointment, place the treats inside the carrier as usual and close the door behind him, secure it and you are good to go. You can now essentially take a piece of your cat's territory with him which he may even find comforting at this stage.

The veterinary clinic

Once you are both at the clinic, you may think things are now out of your hands, however, there are steps you can take to help keep stress to a minimum here too.

- Before you register with a clinic, do your homework to ensure they are conscious of feline welfare as standard. Many practices now have an accreditation that proves they are cat friendly in terms of the set-up of the clinic and handling techniques, so ask about this before joining.
- Some practices have separate waiting rooms for cats and dogs which considerably helps minimise stress. Place your carrier on a table or shelf (if available) as we know they feel safer being up high.
- If there is not a separate waiting area, call the reception from your car and let them know you are waiting there until the appointment time. This may seem like overkill, but dogs are naturally inquisitive, and we can't expect them not to try to approach either to say hello to you, or to inspect your carrier to see what's inside. Some will be excited to see a cat in an already highly emotional situation. Most vets are totally fine with this arrangement – it is better for them if your cat stays as calm as possible as this will help them when performing the examination.
- During the exam itself, if your cat won't come out of his carrier, remove the top half and your vet can do the examination in the carrier where possible. This is

much better than pulling or tipping him out.

- When heading back to reception, if there is no safe space to place your cat while you pay the bill, pop him back in the car first and head back in. Avoid placing him on the floor as he may be easily scared by feet and dogs.

You have the means to make vet visits a much nicer experience for both yourself and your cat. Your cat needs you: set them up for success and make sure you have their back.

Medicating your cat

Lots of people leave the clinic with a box of tablets, filled with dread at the thought of trying to get the medication into their cat. I will take administering twice daily insulin injections to Fig over giving him a tablet any day – and he's the most amenable cat. Many cats are therefore not receiving the treatment they need because they cannot easily be restrained or they spit the tablet out once you have finally got it into their mouth. And because they hide pain so well, it is easy to think they don't need it – but if they do, they do. Please ask your vet or veterinary nurse for help. Ask them to demonstrate how to administer the medication before you leave the clinic if you can. They may have techniques or tools that can help (depending on the type of medication) or there may be another option available that is easier to give (for example, it could be placed on food or injected by your vet or nurse). Let's make sure they get the treatment they deserve in a way that works for both you and your cat.

25

What Your Cat Wants You to Know about Their Later Years

Cats make such wonderful companions, so it's sad that we can only share part of our lives with them. The average lifespan for a domestic cat is thirteen to fourteen years, but it is not uncommon for cats to live well into their late teens or even early twenties. Most cats are considered senior once they are older than ten years of age and most senior diets are suitable for ages seven and above. This means they could be living a significant amount of their life as an older cat and we need to be aware of the changes they go through and how we can accommodate these to maintain good welfare and keep them happy.

Signs of ageing

- Your cat may slow down as she gets older. You may notice she adopts a more sedentary lifestyle and is less keen to go outside, particularly if there are potential stressors outside such as other cats.
- Osteoarthritis is common among older cats, but

can go unnoticed as they conceal it so well. Recent research has found that around 80–90 per cent of cats over the age of ten are affected by arthritis to some degree. That is massive. You may notice her behaviour becomes more hesitant and less free-flowing/fluid. She may hesitate before jumping up or down from a surface, or walk slowly down the stairs rather than trotting down and she may show signs of stiffness in her joints.

- Dental problems are another common ailment among older cats. Sparx recently underwent an operation to have two teeth removed as parts of them had been eroded (tooth resorption). This was picked up at a routine appointment and he was showing no obvious signs of being in any pain or discomfort. Dental issues can cause problems with eating, particularly with dry food, and the pain they experience can be related to any number of behaviour problems including aggression and inappropriate toileting.

- It is common for a cat's kidneys to begin to fail as they age and this is one of the most common reasons cats pass away in old age.

- Your cat may show a reduced tolerance to being handled. She may not enjoy being stroked or picked up any longer as it's painful.

- You may experience changes in how sociable she is. Some cats may want to spend more time with you for reassurance or may prefer to be by themselves and are less likely to seek you out to say hi.

- It is difficult for an older cat to keep up her coat and claw maintenance. She may not be able to reach the lower parts of her body to lick her fur and chew off her back claws. It may be too difficult for her to effectively use a scratch post to keep her front claws short. If they aren't maintained, your cat's front claws can continue to grow and curl round into the paw pad, which is extremely painful and will affect her ability to walk easily.

- Changes to how much they eat and drink. Excessive drinking can be a sign that something is not right and needs to be checked out right away. If she is not able to eat or drink as much as she needs, this will quickly affect her health so, again, keeping in regular contact with your vet is essential.
- Older cats can suffer from cognitive dysfunction, a syndrome similar to dementia that affects their behaviour. This can lead to changes such as confusion, anxiety, restlessness or vocalisation at night and decreased responsiveness to their environment.

How you can help your senior cat

- Your cat may only display some of the symptoms mentioned above as she ages, however, the advice below will help every older cat feel happier in their environment and help them enjoy their old age rather than making it a painful and uncomfortable experience.
- Feed your cat a wet diet that has a high moisture content. This will be easier on her teeth, and will keep her water intake up. Remember to check with your vet for any nutritional advice.

- See your vet for more frequent check-ups. Her health can change at any time and you are unlikely to see any obvious signs until it is very severe. Pain management is crucial for older cats.
- Help them with grooming and claw clipping. If her fur is becoming greasy and unkempt, using a soft brush can help keep it healthy and prevent matting. Clipping the very tips of her claws will prevent them from curling round.
- Avoid making any big changes to your home if you can, including bringing home new cats. Manage existing stressors where possible, for example, teach children not to be too heavy-handed and keep your dog away from her.
- Set up your home for an elderly cat. Make sure she can get to her food, water and into the litter tray. Make life easy for her. Place her food and water near areas she likes to sleep so she doesn't have to wander through the house to get to them. Use steps and smaller platforms to help her access high places without placing additional pressure on her joints. If she loves the space on top of the wardrobe but can't get up there anymore, find a way to help her or make a new high space that's easier for her to reach.
- Provide lots of very soft resting areas. I recently made a cat bed out of a cheap IKEA duvet that I folded and stitched together. It is a lot softer than anything else my cats had previously, and both use it every day and sleep in it through the night.
- Finally, anticipate behavioural changes and find a way to work around them that works for your cat. If

she has always had a high-sided litter tray, it is only natural that this will become difficult for her to get into eventually and she may pee on the carpet instead as it's more comfortable. Try not to get cross, take stock of what is happening and swap for a lower-sided tray.

Euthanasia due to behaviour problems

In my experience, it is uncommon for a cat to be put to sleep solely for their behaviour. There is not the same pressure on aggressive cats as there is on aggressive dogs. Dogs usually need to be taken for walks and the owner is liable for any injuries or damage their dog inflicts, whereas it is not the case for cats, helping to avoid euthanasia.

It also helps that most cats can live a fulfilled life with minimal human contact, so under-socialised or feral cats who are more likely to act aggressively can avoid being around people altogether. The problem is that suitable homes are few and far between – there is not an endless list of people waiting to take on aggressive cats they cannot spend any time with. While waiting for the right home, these cats can spend months or even years in a kennel or pen and this is a miserable life for a feral or long-term stray. Euthanasia may be a kinder option if there is no hope of them being released back into a community to live freely.

In most cases of aggression, with the right management, it can be significantly improved, but this often involves making permanent changes to the environment or the behaviour of the people around them. For example,

I recently met a cat who was taken to the vets to be put to sleep for severely attacking his owner's arm numerous times. The bites and scratches were severe and had required hospital treatment to prevent infection. Thankfully, his vet referred him over to me instead and with just a few (permanent) changes to his owner's behaviour, the aggression stopped entirely, almost instantly.

That being said, there are times aggressive cats cannot live around people without a high risk of aggression. These include confident cats that have previously been abused by people and have learnt to show aggression as part of their normal behaviour. For example, the cat insists on sitting on your lap, but shows severe aggression at your slightest movement and without any warning. Euthanasia may be an option for this cat as he may not cope with living a life away from human interaction altogether, but the risk of injury to the people he lives with would be too great. However, just to be clear, I have never had to recommend euthanasia for aggressive behaviour, even in the most difficult situations, so always consult a behaviourist, alongside your vet, before making any decisions.

Euthanasia due to medical problems

It is truly heartbreaking when your cat comes to the end of her life. Often the responsibility of deciding when our cat's time has come falls to us and the greatest final gift we can give her is to relieve her suffering. But this is so difficult.

Knowing when the right time is, is not easy. Many cats are left too long because they hide their suffering so well.

My feeling is it is better to let them go peacefully a few days (or even weeks) early than a moment too late. We have the chance to give them the perfect end, free of suffering, if we are strong enough to give it to them.

This is so easy for me to say, but the situation is so full of emotion, and I know we would all give so much to spend one more day with a beloved feline companion. Here are some signs that it may be time to say goodbye to your cat:

- She has stopped eating or drinking. If this is happening, your cat needs to see a vet immediately.
- She has become incontinent and no longer has full control of her bladder or bowels.
- She needs medication but administering the tablets or medicine is highly stressful for her.
- She is constantly hiding and will not come out unless essential.
- She shows no interest in life. She may be sleeping, eating, drinking and toileting, but not engaging in any social interactions, or making use of her territory.

It is so difficult to make a judgement call with your own cat. We can only do our best and try to do what is right for them at the time, putting our emotions to the side when we can and asking for help if we need it. Remember, once your cat has been put to sleep, there is no question over her welfare, she will be at rest. If only they really did have nine lives.

CONCLUSION

Working with cats and their people is one of the highlights of my job as a cat behaviourist. Each and every person I meet has their cat's best interest at heart, wants them to be happy and wants to know they are doing all the right things. It makes me smile to know that includes you too, and you have taken the time to join me on this journey to learn more about the mysteries of your cat and their behaviour.

I work closely with my clients, and it is heart warming to see the transformation, not just in their cat's behaviour, but the change in how they feel towards each other. Recently, I worked with a lady who was being attacked by her cat daily. She found this so upsetting and had convinced herself that he hated her. We sat together for a long time and unpicked his behaviour, and realised he was only trying to play (while getting himself into some very bad habits!), and reassured with this knowledge, something clicked. She knew there was no malice there, if anything he liked her the most! This change in mindset gave her the encouragement she needed for additional playtimes and to transform his home into a more stimulating environment. Their relationship was back on track and is flourishing more than ever. If your cat is showing some challenging behaviours or you realise you have made mistakes along the way and things haven't quite turned out how you hoped, don't feel disheartened, we've all been there – myself included – and it's not too late to turn things around. I hope this book leaves you feeling empowered to go out and make the changes you need to give your cat the opportunity to be the best companion they can be, while living their best life. THANK YOU for being in your cat's corner and wanting the very best for them – you really are wonderful.

It has been a joy to write this book for you, a cat lover, and for those yet to discover the truly rewarding experience of sharing life with a cat. Despite popular belief, cats are such loving creatures, and you can make such a difference to their happiness by taking time to understand them. Let's continue to advocate for cats and share the knowledge that is out there – if only everyone was as wonderful as you and took the time to find it.

I hope you have enjoyed reading this book and it makes you love your cat just that little bit more. Give them a little head boop from me.

INDEX

ACKNOWLEDGEMENTS

I would like to give a very heartfelt thank you to the following people who have been instrumental in the creation of this book.

To Pepper, Parker and Marnie, my wonderful children. The way it feels to watch you fall in love with animals – be it cats, dogs, tigers or axolotls – just the way I did is truly heart warming. You make me so proud to be your mum and I hope this book makes you proud of me one day – it is all for you. Finally got to 70,000 words! I love you all.

To Sam, my husband, my best friend and my favourite dog lover. This book just would not be here without you – not just because you encouraged me to swap bedtime routines for Starbucks and a laptop, but for your unwavering confidence and wholehearted faith in me. Thank you for being the best companion for this awesome (and exhausting) adventure we call life. You are an amazing human being and your friendship is more valuable than this life. I love you.

To Lynn Allott, my lovely mum, for starting it all with your love of cats. Because of you I shared my childhood with Tibby and Lily (and more – I couldn't name them all here!) and you inspired me to want to learn so much more about them. You won't learn anything new in these pages, but I know you will read them all anyway. Thank you for always being proud of me, you're the best and I love you.

To Abi, Dan and Lela, dear friends who became family decades ago. Your infinite encouragement in every part of my life means so much and I couldn't be without you all. Thank you for forever believing in me, for always being there and for never letting any feelings of doubt creep in for very long. Everybody needs friends like you guys, I love you all and will always be there for you too.

To Lucy Cruickshanks, for you unwavering support and guidance throughout every step of this process. Your literary knowledge knows no bounds and you always listen and help me with such positivity and humour. But I mostly love you for our shared love of cats, cat memes, cat videos and matching cat-themed Christmas jumpers. I know you always read the acknowledgements first so hello and hi Fluffy, I hope you like it!

To Jessica Duffy, for your passion and enthusiasm for this project, and for supporting my publishing journey with such kindness and patience. Thank you for always being at the end of an email or zoom and providing such invaluable support and advice throughout, it has been a joy to work together.

To Laura McKendry of Bird and Beast, for the wonderful illustrations throughout this book. You have captured the magic and mystery of the cat perfectly and every image is so unique, with its own little character, just like in real life. It is so heart warming to see Fig and Sparx included too, it makes this book just that little bit more special to me.

To the cat behaviour community that is full of supportive, empowering and remarkable people who build each other up and work together to advocate for the welfare of cats. Thank you for the work you do for the behavioural wellbeing of cats across the world, and thank you for the support and encouragement in this amazing but often emotionally challenging industry.

And thank you to you, the reader. For being on your cat's side and for looking to be the best cat person you can be. Your cat is in good hands with you.